Special
Educational
Needs

Also available in the Key Debates in Educational Policy series

Teaching Thinking Skills 2nd edition, Stephen Johnson and
Harvey Siegel, edited by Christopher Winch

Educational Equality, Harry Brighouse, Kenneth R. Howe and
James Tooley, edited by Graham Haydon

Special Educational Needs

A New Look

Mary Warnock
and Brahm Norwich

Edited by
Lorella Terzi

Key Debates in Educational Policy

continuum

Continuum International Publishing Group
The Tower Building
11 York Road
London SE1 7NX

80 Maiden Lane
Suite 704
New York, NY 10038

www.continuumbooks.com

British Library Cataloguing-in-Publication Data
A catalogue record for this book is available from the British Library.

ISBN: 978-1-4411-8015-5 (paperback)

Library of Congress Cataloging-in-Publication Data
Norwich, Bram.
  Special educational needs : a new look / By Bram Norwich and Mary
Warnock, edited by Lorella Terzi.
    p. cm.— (Key debates in educational policy)
  Includes bibliographical references and index.
  ISBN 978-1-4411-8015-5 (pbk.)
  1. Special education—Great Britain. 2. Special education teachers—
Great Britain. I. Warnock, Mary. II. Terzi, Lorella. III. Title. IV. Series.
  LC3986.G7N673 2010
  371.90941—dc22

                              2009047136

Typeset by Ben Cracknell Studios
Printed and bound in Great Britain by the MPG Books Group

Contents

Notes on Contributors

Baroness Warnock is a distinguished philosopher and a prominent figure in education. She has had a remarkable career as a shaper of social policy, and has run a girls' school as well as a Cambridge college. She is well known as the chair of government committees, and she became a Life Peer in 1985. Mary Warnock's books on ethics, education, Sartre and the imagination have been widely read for many years. She has recently published *Easeful Death: Is There a Case for Assisted Dying?* (with Dr Elisabeth Macdonald; Oxford University Press, 2009).

Brahm Norwich is Professor of Educational Psychology and Special Educational Needs at the School of Education and Lifelong Learning, University of Exeter. He has worked as a teacher, a professional educational psychologist and researched and published widely in these fields. His most recent books are *Moderate Learning Difficulties and the Future of Inclusion* (Routledge, 2005), *Special Teaching for Special Children: Pedagogies for Inclusion* (with Ann Lewis; Open University Press, 2004) and *Dilemmas of Difference, Disability and Inclusion: International Perspectives* (Routledge, 2008).

Lorella Terzi is a philosopher of education with training in political and moral philosophy. She is the author of *Justice and Equality in Education: a Capability Perspective on Disability and Special Educational Needs* (Continuum, 2008) which innovatively applies Amartya Sen's capability approach to questions of provision for children with disabilities and special educational needs. She is a Reader at Roehampton University.

Acknowledgements

I am grateful to the distinguished contributors to this collection, Mary Warnock and Brahm Norwich, for their excellent essays and their prompt responses to my suggestions. I admire and respect their positions and consider it a real privilege to have worked with them on this project. Warm thanks are due to Chris Winch, Editor of the Key Debates Series of the Philosophy of Education Society of Great Britain, both for inviting me to edit the volume and for his kind and sustained support. I would also like to thank Alison Clark, Commissioning Editor at Continuum, for her friendly, knowledgeable and patient assistance and Ruth Cigman for her helpful advice. Finally, I am grateful to my many students and my colleagues at Roehampton University for engaging and enriching my ideas.

Lorella Terzi

Series Editor's Preface – Key Debates in Educational Policy

Christopher Winch

Impact pamphlets were launched in 1999 as an initiative of the Philosophy of Education Society of Great Britain. Their aim was to bring philosophical perspectives to bear on UK education policy and they have been written by leading general philosophers or philosophers of education. At the time of writing, 18 have been published.

They deal with a variety of issues relating to policy within the field of education. Some have focused on controversial aspects of current government policy such as those by Andrew Davis on assessment, Harry Brighouse on disparities in secondary education, Mary Warnock on changes in provision for pupils with special educational needs and Colin Richards on school inspection. Others, such as those by Michael Luntley on performance-related pay and by Christopher Winch on vocational education and training, have been critical of new policy initiatives. Yet others have been concerned with the organization and content of the school curriculum. These have included pamphlets by Kevin Williams on the teaching of foreign languages, Steve Bramall and John White on Curriculum 2000, David Archard on sex education, Stephen Johnson on thinking skills, Graham Haydon on personal, social and health education and John Gingell on the visual arts.

The launch of each pamphlet has been accompanied by a symposium for policy makers and others at which issues raised in the pamphlets have been further explored. These have been attended by government ministers, opposition spokespersons, other MPs, representatives from the Qualifications and Curriculum Authority, employers' organizations, trades unions and teachers' professional organizations as well as by members of think tanks, academics and journalists.

  Some of the original pamphlets have made a lasting impression on the world of education policy and have, in addition, sparked debates in both the policy and academic worlds. They have revealed a hunger for dealing with certain topics in a philosophically oriented way because it has been felt that the original pamphlet initiated a debate in a mode of thinking about educational issues that needs and deserves to be taken a lot further. The Key Debates in Educational Policy series aims to take some of these debates further by selecting from those original Impact pamphlets whose influence continues to be keenly felt and either reproducing or expanding them to take account of the most recent developments in the area with which they deal. In addition, each of the original pamphlets receives a lengthy reply by a distinguished figure in the area who takes issue with the main arguments of the original pamphlet. Each of the Key Debates volumes also contains a substantial foreword and/or afterword by an academic with strong interests in the area under discussion, which gives the context and provides extensive commentary on the questions under discussion and the arguments of the original author and his/her respondent.

  There are a number of reasons for doing this. Philosophical techniques applied to policy issues can be very powerful tools for clarifying questions and developing arguments based on ethical, aesthetic, political and epistemological positions. Philosophical argumentation is, however, by its nature, controversial and contested. There is rarely, if ever, one side to a philosophical question. The fact that the Impact pamphlets have often aroused lively debate and controversy is testament to this. There has been a desire for a more rounded version of the debate to be presented in a format accessible to those who do not have a formal philosophical background but who find philosophical argumentation about educational issues to be useful in developing their own ideas. This series aims to cater for this audience while also presenting rigorous argumentation that can also appeal to a more specialist audience.

It is hoped that each volume in this series will provide an introduction and set the scene to each topic and give the readership a splendid example of philosophical argumentation concerning a complex and important educational issue.

Introduction

Lorella Terzi

Provision for children with special educational needs raises important and contentious questions at the level of theory, policy and practice in education. Many of these questions relate directly to the fundamental problem of how best we can enact the equal entitlement of every child to education, while acknowledging and respecting individual differences. They also relate to considerations about the aims of education and the role of schooling in society.

First, for example, is the question of whether or not to identify children's differences and, if so, what differences should be considered relevant to education, and by which means they should be identified and evaluated. The current educational framework in England is based on the identification of children's differences in learning in terms of educational needs. It is recognized that, during their schooling, some children have special educational needs, i.e. needs requiring provision which is additional to, and different from, provision on average available in mainstream schools. However, concerns have been raised about the usefulness of the concept of special educational needs as an appropriate means of identifying and describing children's differences (Norwich, 1993, 1996 and chapter 2 in this volume). Moreover, issues arise in relation to the possible discriminatory and 'labelling' use of the concept, seen by some as inscribed in a model which emphasizes individual differences as 'deficits', thus inherently devaluing children on the basis of their presumed 'defects' (Barton, 2003; Corbett, 1996).

Second is the question of schooling or, more specifically, of whether children should be educated together, in a common 'inclusive' project, or whether they should attend special, or indeed specialist, schools, more 'attuned' to their individual characteristics. This questions is interrelated to conceptions of inclusive education (more on this below), and entails not only considerations about the location of education, but also wider concerns about curricular contents, learning and teaching methods, and teachers' expertise. While current provision in England encompasses both special schools, catering only for children with special educational needs, and mainstream 'inclusive' schools, where these children learn alongside their peers, current policy is mainly geared towards educating children with special educational needs in mainstream schools.

Third, and related to the previous two, is the question of the funding of special needs education, which requires accountable and feasible means of providing appropriately for different needs, together with considerations about fair allocation of resources within limited budgets. The situation in England in this respect is two-fold. It involves a system of identification of needs conducted and funded by schools, alongside a complex and often lengthy process through which Local Authorities issue 'statements of special educational needs'. This process ensures that additional, externally funded services and support are provided for children whose needs are not met through special intervention at school level. However, the complexity of this system has resulted in profoundly unequal resource allocation across Local Authorities, with consistent and widespread differences, both in the number of statements issued, and in terms of funding (Terzi, 2008). It has furthermore caused tensions and disputes between parents, schools and Local Authorities.

Finally, provision for children with special educational needs raises a further, important and deeply controversial question, which fundamentally underpins the previous ones, and concerns the meaning of inclusion in education. While there seems to be a general consensus on the value of inclusion, there is little agreement on what this actually means in an educational context. A project of inclusive education, for instance, is seen by some as a process towards the aim of an inclusive society, where the role of schools is to prepare for participation in social arrangements. On this view, every child should be educated in mainstream schools, which should be flexible and able to effectively respond to differences, without recourse to special provision. Others maintain, instead, that schools should specifically be focused on the characteristics of children and their learning, and hence special schools should be considered part of a broad inclusive project (Cigman, 2007). While these are only some of the questions that characterize debates on special needs education, each of them involves several further problems and points of contention, thus exemplifying the complex nature of the issues involved.

It is against this background that I present the essays of this volume, the main aim of which is to further the debate on provision for children with special educational needs, and to make suggestions for educationalists, policy-makers and politicians. The collection brings together new essays by Baroness Mary Warnock and Brahm Norwich in an interesting and compelling discussion which innovatively engages many of the questions outlined above. Stemming from the ideas expressed in 2005 by Mary Warnock in her thought-provoking pamphlet 'Special Educational Needs: A New Look' – reproduced integrally in this collection – the debate between these two scholars comprises a response by Brahm Norwich to the pamphlet, followed by a further reply by Mary Warnock. The result is a set of different and, at times, contrasting theoretical and more practically oriented insights, which nevertheless suggest important ways forward in the field. A concluding chapter aims at critically tying elements of the debates together. In the following summaries I briefly touch upon some of the insights discussed in each essay, while attempting to present the main elements of contention between the authors.

Undoubtedly, the 1978 Inquiry into the Education of Handicapped Children, chaired by Mary Warnock, and hence known as the Warnock Report, has marked a watershed in the education of children with disabilities, and has established a framework of provision whose main elements are still in place today. In 2005, nearly 30 years after the influential Report, Warnock published a pamphlet, 'Special Educational Needs: A New Look', in which she reflects upon some of the more contentious aspects of the legacy of the 1978 Report. It is within the Report, and indeed its enactment in the 1981 Education Act, she claims, that the 'seeds of confusion', which still characterize the field today, were planted (page 18). According to Warnock, confusion has emerged in relation to the concept of needs, and particularly the statement of special educational needs, as well as in relation to the ideal of inclusion. This confusion, she furthermore argues, reflects elements of the dilemma of difference which, central to current debates, consists in the tension between treating all children as the same (accentuating their 'sameness') or treating them differently (accentuating their individual, special features) (page 15). Warnock maintains that, while being a valuable attempt to avoid 'categorizing' children into fixed disabilities and hence to avoid 'labelling' them, the introduction of the concept of special educational needs has however led to a problematic 'tendency to refer to children with very different needs as if they were all the "same", i.e. special educational needs (SEN) children' (page 19).

Furthermore, the unspecified nature of the concept has resulted in a set of unclear criteria for determining entitlement to a statement of special educational needs, and has ultimately led to a complex and uneven system of provision, 'so that children with much the same needs may get entirely different provision' (pages 24–5).

Finally, Warnock claims that the concept of inclusion, understood as the right of each child to be educated in a mainstream school or 'under the same roof', constitutes a 'disastrous legacy', in that it has resulted in many children being physically included in, but essentially emotionally excluded from, a common project of learning (pages 19 and 32). This situation, she claims, is particularly evident in the case of children with emotional and behavioural needs and for those with autism, as well as for children with needs arising from social disadvantage (who were, however, not originally considered in the Report). In Warnock's view, for these children, as for many others whose needs remain unmet in mainstream schools, the project of inclusion should be reconsidered, and should entail the possibility of attending special schools. Thus, in what is a critical re-examination of these concepts, interlocked with more practice-based suggestions, Warnock proposes that the statement, together with the process of issuing it, should be reviewed and, if not abolished, it should at least be reconsidered as a 'passport' to special schools (page 32). These should be small, appropriate specialist schools where children could learn and truly experience a feeling of belonging. It is the latter, she continues, that should inform the concept of inclusion. Hence inclusive education should not mean being educated 'under the same roof', as the current 'ideology' has it, but should instead consist in 'being involved in a common enterprise of learning', wherever one can learn best (page 32).

These main themes constitute the bases for Brahm Norwich's response to Warnock. Starting from an account of the vast array of reactions that the pamphlet provoked, from articles in the press and academic papers to political responses, Norwich critically examines key positions and arguments expressed by several commentators, and he refutes some of the interpretations advanced. In particular, he refutes positions claiming that in 2005 Warnock made a historical u-turn on the issue of educating children with special educational needs in mainstream schools. Norwich shows how the original Report envisaged a role for special schools and never implied their complete closure. He further refers to some of Warnock's personal critical stances on the idea of educating all children in the mainstream, dating as back as the early 1990s. This is an important and necessary clarification, which helps in situating the debate within rigorous parameters and in 'clearing the air' of controversial and sensationalist points. But Norwich's analysis goes further, and addresses some of Warnock's ideas which, in his view, require more critical scrutiny, both in the light of theory and of current policies.

First, Norwich maintains that the concept of special educational needs, in the original Report, does recognize 'gradations of needs' (page 60), and has moreover helped in switching the focus from categories based on children's difficulties to a unified category based on required additional provision (pages 84 and 94). This, in his view, is the main contribution of the Report in relation to the concept of special educational needs, rather than the attempt to abandon the use of categories. Secondly, Norwich notices how Warnock's critical stance on the statement of needs reflects a growing concern about its usefulness, and acknowledges the tensions originated by the current system. However, he also argues that Warnock's new suggestion to use statements as 'passports' to special schools, in entailing a completely different function for the statement, would inherently change the nature of the process itself (page 73). Finally, Norwich challenges some of Warnock's critical positions on the ideal of inclusion, and asks whether these amount to a 'closing down on a separatist resolution' (page 74) without a necessary analysis of the value of the 'common school' ideal and the possibility of enacting it through appropriate policy and reforms. On these bases, Norwich outlines his suggestions in relation to each of the points critically addressed. Hence, in his view, the concepts of special educational needs should be reviewed and a new formulation in terms of functional difficulties in education should be considered. He furthermore proposes an articulated framework, including various possible options for the role of statements, from a system based on the concept of additional needs, as used in Scotland, to a two-tier system which would entail both additional provision without statement and the possibility to access the 'statementing' process, if necessary. The adoption of any of these alternative schemes, Norwich claims, would nevertheless require a comprehensive and coordinated system at national and local level. Finally, Norwich articulates and defends his conception of inclusion in education in terms of a pluralistic framework based on the values of individual respect and equality. These two values, in his view, give expression at once to elements of difference (the respect of individual characteristics) and of sameness (the promotion of the sense of belonging to a community), thus moving towards a resolution of the dilemma of difference (page 102). This pluralistic framework should furthermore find expression in an educational system based on a continuum of provision, from differentiated arrangements to more inclusive ones, with the aim of placing the emphasis on elements of commonality and inclusivity. Norwich concludes by stating that, in his view, the future of additional educational provision, rather than in isolation or separately, has to be seen as interrelated to 'a transformed general system' (page 109).

In agreement with Norwich's conclusion, in her reply Mary Warnock cogently presses for a reconsideration of two recommendations originally included in her pamphlet. First, Warnock calls once more for a comprehensive re-examination of special needs education, in place of the piecemeal reforms advocated by the government. A new Committee of Inquiry, according to Warnock, should urgently be established to carry out investigations on several aspects of the current system, and to make recommendations for a much needed radical change (page 119). Second, endorsing Norwich's position, Warnock insists that such investigations should not be carried out separately, because questions of special needs education have to be considered inherently part of questions about education as a whole. Underpinning these points is Warnock's conviction, reinstated in her reply, that evidence-based analysis is essential to inform decisions about education, and particularly about the controversies arising from the dilemmatic nature of special needs provision. According to Warnock, two main aspects of the current educational system should be the subjects of a new inquiry: secondary schooling and primary teaching. Warnock maintains that the shortcomings of current secondary education, characterized by a narrow academically oriented curriculum, which prevents many from achieving, as well as a stifling system of differentiated school-leaving qualifications, should be addressed through appropriate major changes. Warnock favours many of the recommendations expressed by the 2004 Tomlinson Report (in her view, disastrously rejected by the government), including a broader curriculum, encompassing theoretical and more vocational subjects, as well as a new style of teaching and learning, and a unified system of final qualifications. Changes in these directions, according to Warnock, would enormously benefit not only students with special educational needs, but all students. Furthermore, Warnock argues for the importance of good teaching of basic skills at primary school level (page 123), and for the necessity to revise current initial teacher training in order to equip future teachers with more appropriate knowledge and expertise. Finally, Warnock maintains that implementing such changes would help in diminishing the number of children deemed to have special educational needs. This consideration leads her to discuss two of the main points of controversy raised by Norwich, i.e. the concept of special educational needs as a framework-concept, and the question of inclusion. While being deeply interrelated, Warnock notices, both these issues express elements of the dilemma of difference and hence entail no easy solutions. And even if she considers different possibilities, Warnock seems convinced that the concept of special educational needs should after all be retained, together with a system of statements that would allow access to special schools for those children with the most severe needs. Finally, Warnock further expresses her reservation about the concept of inclusion as a social value, but even more so as an educational value, thus clarifying and reinstating the critical stance forcefully expressed in her pamphlet. She concludes by calling once more for evidence-based analysis in order to counteract what she considers to be the dogmatic nature of current positions.

As these summaries indicate, the contributions in this volume advance the debate on special needs education on fundamental theoretical and more policy-oriented issues. Some of these questions, such as the use of concepts to identify differences in education, the role of schools in society and the value of inclusion, as well as the relation between ideals and their enactment in practice, are further analysed in my concluding notes. Notwithstanding their divergent positions on several issues, however, one crucial point importantly unifies the contributions to this volume, i.e. the conviction that questions about special needs education strike at the core of fundamental educational questions and should therefore be considered central and essential to any educational debate.

References

Barton, L. (2003), *Inclusive Education and Teacher Education: a Basis for Hope or a Discourse of Delusion*. London: Institute of Education.

Cigman, R. (ed.) (2007), *Included or Excluded? The Challenge of the Mainstream for Some SEN Children*. London: Routledge.

Corbett, J. (1996), *Bad Mouthing: The Language of Special Needs*. London: Falmer Press.

Department of Education and Science (1978), *Special Educational Needs* (The Warnock Report), London: HMSO.

Department for Education and Skills (2004), *14–19 Curriculum and Qualifications Reform: Final Report of the Working Group on 14–19 Reform* (The Tomlinson Report). Annesley: DfES Publications.

Norwich, B. (1993), 'Has "Special Educational Needs" Outlived it Usefulness?' in Visser, J. and Upton, G. (1993), *Special Education in Britain after Warnock*. London: David Fulton Publishers.

Norwich, B. (1996), 'Special Needs Education, Inclusive Education or Just Education for All?' (Inaugural Lecture). Institute of Education, University of London.

Terzi, L. (2008), *Justice and Equality in Education: A Capability Perspective in Disability and Special Educational Needs*. London and New York: Continuum.

Warnock, M. (2005), *Special Educational Needs: A New Look*. London: Philosophy of Education Society of Great Britain, Impact Series N.11.

Special Educational Needs: A New Look[1]

Mary Warnock

Overview

The 1972 Education Act gave all children a right to education, however severe their disabilities. The concept of the ineducable child was abolished, and new principles of universal education were needed. The Committee of Inquiry into the Education of Handicapped Children and Young People was set up in 1974 with a view to establishing such principles, and its conclusions formed the basis of the Education Act 1981. I was chairman of this committee and I believe that, more than 30 years on, it is time for a radical review.

Special needs education, along with the pivotal concept of the statement of special educational need, has recently been subjected to serious criticism. Much of it is justified, and I would go further in this direction than many critics. In particular I would challenge the widely held view that, for all the problems in special needs education today, the statement should be retained as a 'safety net'. There is in my view a crucial lack of clarity in the concept of a statement, and while this continues to be so it is all but useless as a safety net. This lack of clarity has two aspects, one related to the concept of need, the other related to the concept of inclusion.

The statement of special educational need was seen in contrast to the medical model, according to which some children are 'normal', others are 'handicapped'. Our idea was that there are common educational goals – independence, enjoyment and understanding – towards which *all* children, irrespective of their abilities or disabilities, should aim. We suggested that for some children the path towards these goals was smooth and easy, whereas for others it was beset by obstacles. Some children *needed* help in overcoming these obstacles. They encountered special difficulties on the path towards the common goals. Every human being has certain needs and difficulties, so this approach was inclusive rather than exclusive. Statements conferred a right to special provision on the children who received them, and imposed a corresponding duty on their Local Authorities to provide it. This was well and good, except that the criteria for deciding who should have a statement were never clear. The concept of need covers a wide spectrum: we say that a person who is severely dehydrated *needs water*, and also that a person whose car has broken down *needs a new one*. Whereas it was clear that severely disabled children *needed* special help, this was less clear with some of the milder disabilities, which might nevertheless prevent a child from learning successfully unless help was forthcoming. The lack of clarity was reflected in the fact that our original guess of how many children would receive statements was wildly off the mark. We thought the figure would be around 2 per cent. The actual figure was around 20 per cent.

Not only is there a gradation of needs which our early thinking did not adequately address, there is also a wide range of different *kinds* of need covered by the statement. Some needs (those of dyslexic children, for example) could usually be successfully met in mainstream classrooms. Others (those of children with autistic disorders or behavioural problems) were hard, if not impossible, to meet in this way. The concept of inclusion was taking a foothold in society generally. This meant that there was a tendency to overlook the differences not only between the educationally 'needy' and others, but also between various *kinds* of educational need.

The issue of mainstream versus special education is crucial. The inclusive ideology came to mean that, not only did statemented children have a right to special provision, they also had a right to be 'included' in mainstream schools, provided that they did not adversely affect the learning of others. This last proviso has been highly problematic, since an adverse effect on learning can be hard to prove. Since 2002, heads and governors have been liable to a criminal charge if they exclude a disruptive child from a mainstream school against the wishes of the parent. Yet it seems clear that disruptive children frequently hinder teaching and learning.

Special needs expert, Alan Dyson, has argued that there is a fundamental contradiction in the UK educational system between 'an intention to treat all learners as essentially the same and an equal and opposite intention to treat them as different' (Dyson, 2001). I believe that he is right, and this means that, at the heart of our thinking about education, there is confusion of which children are the casualties. The desire to 'include' children in single institutions is a desire to treat them as the same, and though this is a worthy ideal, it can be carried too far. For children are also different, and it is essential to acknowledge this, since refusal to address genuine differences can wholly undermine our attempts to meet children's needs. This, I believe, is what we are seeing today, and the way forward is for the government to set up another commission to review the situation.

One possibility would be the setting up of special (or 'specialist') schools based on a new concept of inclusion. Instead of the simplistic ideal of including all children 'under the same roof', we should consider the ideal of including all children in the common educational enterprise of learning, *wherever they can learn best*. There are some needs (for example, those of children suffering from autism and those of many children in care) which are more *effectively* met in separate institutions, where the children are known well by their teachers and are not as vulnerable to bullying as they inevitably are in mainstream schools. There is a case for setting up a kind of school that is small and caters not for children with the most severe disabilities, but for those whose disabilities prevent them from learning in the environment of a large school. Such schools could be respected centres of learning. They could specialize in subjects like the Performing Arts or IT, and be open to the wider community in the evenings or at weekends. Statements could then serve a new and important purpose, as a kind of passport of entry. In other words, a statement would confer a *right* to attend a specialist school, and because such schools would be attractive to the wider community, parents would come to seek entry for their children, who would be properly included within their school.

Indeed small specialist schools of the kind described would be inclusive in an important sense of the word for children who currently suffer from feelings of exclusion within mainstream schools. The concept of inclusion must embrace the *feeling of belonging*, since such a feeling appears to be necessary both for successful learning and for more general well-being. I believe that small specialist schools could engender this feeling for many children who now lack it; but hard evidence is needed to support this view. A new review of special needs provision would have the important function of collecting and analyzing such evidence.

Mary Warnock
April 2005

1. The historical background

In this section I explore the legal and conceptual history of special education over the last few decades, indicating where, in my opinion, difficulties have arisen. I discuss the Education Acts of 1972, 1981 and 1988, and look at the tension in government policy between treating all learners as the same and treating them as different.

Special education in Britain has been locked for over three decades into the framework set out in the Education Act of 1981. This act introduced statements for children with special educational needs, and imposed a duty on LEAs to provide for such children as specified by their statements. I want to suggest that now, more than 30 years after the Committee of Inquiry whose report led to the 1981 Act was set up, it is time for another government commission to re-examine the provision currently available, and especially the assumptions upon which the present framework is based. I shall examine the key concepts of the 1981 Act, first the concept of need, and second the concept of inclusion, formerly known as integration. Special needs expert, Alan Dyson, has argued that there is a fundamental contradiction in education systems in the UK between 'an intention to treat all learners as essentially the same and an equal and opposite intention to treat them as different' (Dyson, 2001). I believe that he is right, and that this contradiction puts great strain on any attempt to produce a coherent policy for special education.

In order to justify my claim that nothing less than a radical revolution is now required I shall have to begin with an historical survey. The starting point is the Committee of Inquiry into the Education of Handicapped Children and Young People, established by Margaret Thatcher as Secretary of State for Education, and taken on by the Labour government of 1974. This committee started work in the summer of 1974. One of the reasons for setting it up was that, two years earlier, legislation had been introduced giving all children an entitlement to education, however severe their disabilities, and abolishing the category of the 'ineducable child'. Since 1972, then,

Local Education Authorities had been struggling without much systematic guidance to provide school education, mostly in existing special schools, for the most severely disabled with whom they had not had to tangle before. A new principle of genuinely universal education had to be formulated.

Thus our task as a committee was first of all to articulate a concept of education that could make sense in the context of any child, anywhere on the continuum of ability or disability. We envisaged a common set of goals, independence, enjoyment and understanding, that should be seen as common to all children. The path towards these goals was smooth and easy for some, but beset with all kinds of obstacles for the children who were our concern. The provision of education for the so-called 'handicapped' should therefore be seen as the gradual removing of obstacles, or provision of help in overcoming them, so that progress, however limited, could be made towards the common goals. Hence we came to think not so much about what was wrong with a child, as about what he would need if he were to make progress. It was out of this vision of shared educational goals that the concept of special needs arose.

The figures supplied to us by the Department showed that children whose educational needs were special were by no means confined to the 2 per cent or so who were being educated in special schools. It was suggested that, besides these, there were approximately 18 per cent in ordinary classrooms in mainstream schools who, at some time or other in their school career, would need extra help, or who were in need of special equipment to enable them to take part in education. The variety of needs within this total of 20 per cent was of course enormous.

In some ways these figures helped us to realize one of our aims, which was to normalize special education. We could point to the fact that many children with special needs ('handicapped' children) were already in mainstream schools, being helped, more or less, to keep up with the ordinary curriculum. Being recognized as having a special educational need did not entail that a child suddenly became a member of a race apart, deserving of an entirely different kind of education from that of his contemporaries.

In attempting to concentrate attention on the means that schools could take to remove or reduce the obstacles a child might encounter in his learning, we thought we should try to move away from the medical model of diagnosis, that is of identifying a child as having a certain named condition such as 'mental subnormality' or 'maladjustment' (the two categories of disability that together made up by far the majority of the 20 per cent). We hoped that, in identifying what needed to done be to help a child to learn, schools could adopt a neutral tone regarding the child's deficiencies, instead calling the attention of parents and others to what some extra help would enable him to do. They might say 'he needs specialist help with his speech and language', for example; or 'he needs lots of practice with his physical coordination'. In this way we hoped to emphasize the seamless continuum of abilities and needs found within the ordinary classroom and treat all learners, in Alan Dyson's words, as essentially the same.

At the same time, mindful of the needs of those hitherto held to be ineducable, we wanted to protect the interests of those who had the most severe and complex educational difficulties, so that in the enthusiasm for 'normalizing' special needs, we would not allow those children to slip back into the position where they received no education, because their education could never approach the normal. We therefore invented the statement of special educational need. This was to be a document issued by the Local Authority, after expert assessment of a child's abilities and disabilities, which would list the extra support that he would need in order to make progress, the provision of which would be a statutory duty laid on the Local Authority. We hoped that a child with a statement could carry it with him if he moved to a different part of the country; and it could be taken into account if, for example, he had to go into hospital.

Most of these relatively benign aspirations were embodied in the 1981 Education Act. The good that came out of them was that, as many parents and teachers testified, it became much easier than before to admit that children had many different special needs and that having such a need did not make a child a freak. Teachers themselves became more interested in undertaking training so that they would be able to recognize and meet these needs, and the meeting of special needs in mainstream schools became gradually better organized, with school governors as well as teachers taking responsibility. There was some kind of climate change, at least for a time.

The 1981 Act made no provision for extra funds to be allocated for the new procedures, such as assessment and the issuing of statements (soon to be known as 'statementing'), or for the employment of new, appropriately trained teachers in mainstream schools, even though many special schools were being closed. Indeed, 1981 was almost the worst time that this legislation could have gone onto the Statute Book. It was, after all, drafted in the spirit of 1944, of post-war welfarism. That a need could be demonstrated was taken to be a sufficient justification for the state's meeting it. The act could be seen as a kind of coda to the Butler Act of 1944. (The Butler Act required Local Education Authorities to provide free education to all children – with the exception of those who were held to be ineducable because of their disabilities – up to the age of 15). But 1981 was also the year when educational cuts began to bite. We were moving rapidly away from the idea of education as an intrinsic good to which all were entitled towards the idea of education as a means of producing an improved economy. Before long, the bleak contradiction between the 1981 Act and what was grandiloquently known as The Great Educational Reform Act of 1988 became manifest.

However, apart from the fact that the 1981 Act was ill-timed, for which perhaps no one can be blamed, it also contained the seeds of confusion which, I fear, can be traced back to the 1978 Report of the Committee of Inquiry, and which in my view still bedevils the field of special educational needs to this day. First, the desire to avoid categories of disability into which children could be slotted and in which they would possibly remain indefinitely, led to a tendency to refer to children with very different needs as if they were all the 'same', i.e. special educational needs (SEN) children. This fear of 'labelling' children by referring to them by the categories into which they fell was part of a very general movement in society as a whole (the beginning, perhaps, of political correctness) to avoid words like 'deaf' or 'blind', in favour of phrases like 'people with hearing difficulties' (which supposedly remind us that we are all people and are all subject to difficulties of various kinds.) Despite the fact that such language is cumbersome, it fitted well with the committee's determination to widen the scope of the idea of the 'special', including within it many children already being taught in mainstream schools, but needing more support than they were getting at the time.

However, the idea of transforming talk of disability into talk of what children need if they are to make progress has turned out to be a baneful one. If children's needs are to be assessed in public discussion and met by public expenditure it is absolutely necessary to have ways of identifying not only what is needed but also why (by virtue of what condition or disability) it is needed. It is essential, furthermore, to distinguish needs that radically differ from one another, arising from different disabilities. It is hopelessly muddled to treat a need for, say, ramps to allow access to laboratories for a physically disabled child as comparable with a need for constant supervision for a young Down's Syndrome child who is prone to run away. The implications for the resources of the school are totally different, and I shall argue that the failure to distinguish various kinds of needs has been disastrous for many children.

The concept of the statement of special needs is beset with confusion. Section 2 will be devoted to this topic; and I now want to move on to what is possibly the most disastrous legacy of the 1978 Report, the concept of inclusion (formerly known as integration). Like an inheritance that grows and becomes more productive from one generation to another, this concept has gained a remarkable foothold in our society.

In the context of educational policy, what people (including ministers) think about the inclusion of children with special needs in mainstream schools cannot be separated from what they think is the proper function of special schools. At the present time, the official attitude to special schools is patronizing. We are told that, sadly, they have to continue in existence, and even that they have a valuable role for those children with the most severe and complex disabilities. They are, in effect, to be regarded as little more than places of containment, hospitals or 'day centres', but with better educational facilities, whose expertise may, with luck, spill over into the mainstream where special needs children properly belong. Such attitudes as these formed a kind of subterranean stream in the deliberations of the 1974 committee, a stream which every now and then surfaced and flowed quite strongly above ground. Some members of the committee openly espoused the ideal of ultimately doing away with special schools altogether, on the ground that comprehensive education could not be held to have succeeded until all children whatever their abilities were educated in them together. Any segregation according to ability was thought to be disastrously elitist, and this applied as much to segregating SEN children in special schools as it did to segregating the most able in grammar schools. This was the ideology of inclusion.

I have already mentioned the Education Act of 1988, which was one of the most far-reaching of the century. This act put the National Curriculum in place, and inaugurated the league tables in which schools would compete against each other according to their academic results. As far as children with disabilities were concerned, the concept of educational need had been virtually dropped from the agenda. Whatever children might need, what they got was supposed to be an education fitting them for work in industry. But the assumption that most SEN children would receive their education in mainstream schools was not questioned.

Paradoxically, though a National Curriculum was introduced, and children were to be tested on it at various stages along the way, the system of broadly speaking academic external examinations, GCSE and A level, according to which schools were to be judged and awarded their place in the league tables remained virtually unchanged. True success lay in academic success at A levels. The least academically able children were doomed to fail by these criteria; worse, they would drag their schools down with them by lowering their ranking in the tables. Competition was to govern educational provision; and in the proper spirit of the market schools that had the least success (partly, in many cases, because they had a large number of children with special needs) were to be allowed to 'wither away'. Choice was supposed to produce higher academic standards. It was never clear what was to happen to the unfortunate children who attended the least successful schools during the process of withering, nor where they might subsequently be welcome. The greater the pressure to raise academic standards, the worse the fate of those who could never shine according to such standards.

Partly in an attempt to redress the balance in favour of children with disabilities, while adhering to the principle of 'integration', the early 1990s saw the introduction of an elaborate code of practice, according to which children in mainstream schools should have their needs assessed in various stages and be given extra help either within the ordinary resources of the school, or from outside, and given a statement if their needs appeared to warrant it. Every school now had to appoint someone as a special educational needs coordinator (or SENCO), whose responsibility it was to ensure that all the procedures of assessment and statementing were properly followed. An appeal system was set in place by which parents could have their complaints heard and disputes with Local Education Authorities could be settled. It was the presumption of the code that children identified as having special needs should stay at their mainstream school if that was what their parents wanted. In 1993 an education act reached the Statute Book which sought to ensure that both LEAs and school governors should have regard to this code of practice. The Special Educational Needs and Disability Act 2001 provided a revised statutory framework for inclusion, strengthening the right of children with special needs to attend mainstream schools if their parents wished it and if their inclusion did not adversely affect other pupils in the school. And alongside this, the Disability Discrimination Act 2001 placed a new duty on schools not to treat disabled pupils less favourably than others, and to make reasonable adjustments to ensure that they were not disadvantaged. The following year a new code of practice was issued, to take account of the new legislation.

One of the requirements most insisted on in the 1978 Report and in the 1981 legislation was that different departments of government, and especially of local government, health, social services and education should work together in the interests of children. Such collaboration, astonishingly difficult to achieve, is essential in the case of children with special needs. Since the 1990s there have been serious efforts to make this collaboration a reality, though with varying degrees of success. There have been two children acts concerned with the broad issue of children's well-being and rights; and the 2004 Education Act provides that school inspectors, operating a new system of short inspections, should take cognisance not only of narrowly educational matters but matters of general well-being too. This act is especially focused on the need to break down so-called 'organizational barriers' between one profession and another. But schools themselves are given no statutory duty to cooperate with any of the agencies that have responsibility for the well-being of the child; and this is a serious weakness in the legislation. However the flurry of legislation and institutional reform and published strategies, whether they succeed or not, reflects a gradual but significant change of attitude in society towards special education and its role.

When the Committee of Inquiry was set up in 1974 there were two warnings we were given by the then Department of Education. The first was that we were not to include dyslexia as constituting a special need. This was because at the time dyslexia was thought to be a fancy invention of the middle classes to conceal the fact that some of their children were too stupid to be able to learn to read and write or perhaps calculate. This did not matter to us much because, as I have said, our aim was to avoid labelling children as suffering from a named condition but instead to concentrate on what they needed in order to make progress. In the case of dyslexic children their needs are manifest, though not easy to meet. (Incidentally, the case of dyslexia is an example of how 'labelling' inevitably creeps back. Many children are openly described as 'dyslexic' nowadays. Officially they are known as 'children with specific learning difficulties', a phrase intended to replace 'dyslexic', which was a word barred from the civil service vocabulary. But whatever words are used, every school recognizes the condition and arranges specialist help for children who need it.)

The second warning from the Department of Education was more important. We were not to count among children with special educational needs those who suffered from nothing except social deprivation or those for whom, when they started school, English was not their first language.

The latter prohibition arose from the fact that there was a scheme by which the Home Office was supposed to fund the teaching of English as a second language. The Department of Education did not want the responsibility charged to their funds. Moreover because to be called 'a child with special educational needs' was still thought derogatory it was believed that to impute this status to someone solely on the ground that he was not a native English speaker would be offensively racist.

The prohibition against counting social deprivation as giving rise to special educational need arose, I suppose, from the belief embedded in the Department of Education that the social conditions in which a child lived, his background and family, his wealth or poverty, were matters for the Social Services not for them. True educational equality, it was held, could be achieved only if schools treated all children as equally educable, each a tabula rasa upon which good teaching could make its redeeming marks. Of course there are merits in this view, and a kind of nobility. When he was Secretary of State for Education in Margaret Thatcher's government, the unfortunate John Patten caused an uproar when he said that a child's background was totally irrelevant to his educational potential. One can see what he meant: teachers certainly must not assume that a deprived child will never be a high-achiever any more than that the child of an Etonian always will be. But the facts speak for themselves: it is undeniable that socially deprived children tend to have more educational difficulties than children who are not socially deprived. For the first group, school must offer a form of compensation.

The consequence of this embargo was that the Committee could not go as far as it would have liked in advocating special provision for children whose home lives were impoverished, financially, emotionally or linguistically. We certainly advocated an increase in nursery education, but this was based on the principle that 'proper' educational needs could be earlier identified there, rather than the idea that nurseries might supply what socially deprived homes did not.

This refusal to count social deprivation among the causes of special educational need is embedded firmly in the 1981 Act. It looks perfectly absurd today. We all recognize now that children suffer as potential learners from all kinds of deprivation, material and emotional. That is why, at last and belatedly, the special educational needs of children in care, so-called looked-after children, are beginning to be taken seriously. And that is also why the government, to its credit, is supporting Sure Start and other early educational provision. However, the connection between deprivation and educational failure, though now widely recognized, is extremely complex. This, in my view, is an important part of the case for rethinking the concept of special educational needs.

2. The statement of special educational needs reconsidered

In this section I explain why I believe that the statement of special educational need should be reviewed. The criteria for determining who is entitled to a statement are unclear, so that children with much the same needs may get entirely different provision. The present system is both needlessly bureaucratic and liable to cause bad blood between parents, schools and LEAs. Children will lose out so long as these problems persist.

One of the reasons why it seems to me essential to consider again the foundations of public policy on special educational needs is that all the elements in the system hang together. Piecemeal reforms are no longer enough. In the examination of what has gone wrong, I shall start with the statements of special educational need.

The question to whom and for what purpose statements are issued also locks into that of the nature and the functions accorded to special schools. This in turn connects with the policy of inclusion. One could begin anywhere in this interconnected web of problems. But I want to begin with statements, if only because they were an idea that issued directly from the 1970s Committee of Inquiry, so I personally feel a degree of responsibility for what has turned out to be not a very bright idea.

As I have explained, statements of special educational need were proposed by the Committee of Inquiry as a way to protect the interests of those children who had only recently been accorded the right to education of any kind, those with the most severe and often multiple disabilities, such as children with rapidly progressive diseases, children who were most severely brain damaged, or children who were both blind and deaf. Once it had been acknowledged that these children, along with all others, had a legal right to education, most would be in special schools. According to the 1981 Education Act, Local Education Authorities would have a statutory obligation to meet the needs of such children, as specified on the statement. They could never again be deprived of the specific special education that was their right by law. In Scotland the same system was in place, but the statement was known as a record of need.

In the 1970s, about 2 per cent of children of school age attended special schools. Some of these were for children who were severely or multiply disabled or who had severe learning difficulties, but there were many special schools, both independent and maintained, for those with moderate learning difficulties and for 'maladjusted' children, many of whom would have been excluded from mainstream schools. After 1981 many of these latter schools were closed, the special school population being increasingly composed of the most severely physically and intellectually disabled. While it was plain that these children would be issued with statements it was never clear who else would merit one. Which children, among those whose special needs had been identified and who were not in special schools, would be statemented? Parents could on the whole be confident that if their child were attending a special school some effort would be made to meet his needs. What they demanded was assurance that he would have his needs met equally in the maintained school which he was now entitled to attend. It is not surprising that parents began to fight local Authorities to get statements for their children.

The Code of Practice (DfE, 1994), setting out the procedures for identifying special needs in mainstream schools and the various stages of meeting these needs, was not clear on the crucial question of how many of these procedures could be expected to result in a statement. In practice, the number of children issued with statements varied enormously from one Local Education Authority to another. Meanwhile, throughout the 1980s and 1990s the financial position of Local Education Authorities worsened. This had two effects on the practice of statementing. First, as I have suggested, many parents demanded statements for their children because they knew that Local Authorities had a statutory duty to meet needs that were set out in a statement, but not to meet needs that fell short of this. Second, in a situation of scarcity Local Authorities had the desperate task of stretching their resources to cover the needs of all children and, although some extra money came to children with statements, it was not enough. So they began to regard statements as essentially concerned with available resources, not with needs. That is, they specified on the statement what extra support they thought they could afford, regardless of what was in fact needed. This inevitably led to conflict with parents. Tribunals to adjudicate in these disputes were established in 1992, and a painful and extremely long, drawn out process often began, frequently dragging on for months before the child at the centre of it could get any help at all. Local Authority officials, who could hardly be regarded as disinterested, chaired the tribunals, and teachers were not encouraged to give evidence which might involve their employers in expenditure they could not afford. It was no wonder that parents came to feel that all the cards were stacked against them and their children.

Local Authorities were faced with an impossible task. It would be easy to allow expenditure on special needs to use up a disproportionate and inequitable part of the total budget. The children's needs might be great, but so were the needs of all other children at school, including the needs of highly able children or, say, children who were musically gifted. And far too much of the expenditure on special needs was taken up with the bureaucracy of assessments and reassessments, to say nothing of disputes and tribunals.

Meanwhile, following in the footsteps of their predecessors, the Labour government has moved far in the direction of granting autonomy to individual schools, thus stripping LEAs of what was their most valuable function, namely to hold in view the requirements of the whole of their area, and to coordinate and share activities and services between different schools in that area, so that, for example, special needs support staff or peripatetic music teachers could be deployed fairly and where they were most needed. Now that schools employ their own staff and manage their own budgets they inevitably pursue what they see as their own best interests. And this fragmentation of the system has, perhaps paradoxically, gone along with an increased centralization of the control of educational spending. How much schools will get per pupil depends on how well the school is doing according to central criteria; and it is now proposed that how much will be spent on children with special needs will also be determined centrally, and funded by a ringfenced grant. Local Authorities who, at their best, used to know and care for the children for whom they were responsible are visibly withering away. Ministers say that now they are to have an 'enabling' function. It does not seem to amount to much.

It might, however, be argued that increasing centralization and uniformity of policy would at any rate go some way to mitigating the patchiness of provision that at present prevails, and the wide differences between different Authorities in the number of statements they issue. This may be so; but the true evils of the present system, its profligacy both of time and money, its tendency to antagonize parents, will not be remedied until central government can consider again what statements are supposed to be for, and more generally how money ringfenced for the benefit of children with special needs ought to be spent and how it should be divided between those with and those without statements. And this brings me to the role of special schools and their relation to statements.

At the present time all children in special schools have statements; but not all children with statements are in special schools. The statutory framework for inclusion, published by the government in 2001, gave all statemented children a strengthened right to a place in a mainstream school unless that would be incompatible with the wishes of their parents, or with the provision of efficient education of other children in the school (DfES, 2001). For example, many children who are dyslexic have statements specifying what extra help they need, and often they manage to keep up quite well in mainstream schools, provided they get the support they are promised. Many children, too, diagnosed with Asperger's (that is autism at the mild end of the spectrum) have statements and remain in mainstream schools, sometimes successfully. Some children with behavioural problems have statements, and if they become too disruptive to be contained in their mainstream school the LEA is obliged to find alternative ways of educating them.

There are other children who have the same disabilities but who do not have statements, though perhaps the support they get within the school is much the same. However in their case the LEA may change the amount of support without being in breach of the law, and may allow them to be excluded from school with no clear duty to find them suitable alternative education. In practice this is a muddle and, because support for children in mainstream school is so patchy and subject to arbitrary change, teachers and parents are constantly at war with the LEA, and valuable time is wasted for children who badly need continuity in their education, and can ill afford delays and uncertainty.

Meanwhile government thinking seems to be set on immovable tracks. Special schools are places of last resort, only, we are told, for children with 'severe and complex disabilities'. But for other children the aim must be to keep them out of special schools, and by hook or by crook try to educate them in mainstream schools. This is the ideal of inclusion. Because special schools are regarded in this light, parents are understandably anxious to save their children from being sent there. Many parents dread seeing their child relegated to a school which has the most severely mentally disabled pupils, for whom there can be no realistic expectation that they will make educational progress that would be recognized as such in the outside world (crucially important though it is for these individual children that they should progress along the path inch by inch). They know that their Down's Syndrome child, for example, is not as intellectually disabled as these others, and that he will regress if he has no classmates who are brighter than he, and even come to imitate those who are severely disabled. Moreover they see attendance at a special school as a badge of dishonour, and liable to expose their child to jibes and abuse.

There is increasing evidence that the ideal of inclusion, if this means that all but those with the most severe disabilities will be in mainstream schools, is not working. In primary schools, things are not so bad as a rule, provided that the needed support is actually forthcoming. Young children can be very accommodating to the idiosyncrasies of others, and teachers tend on the whole to stay with their class, and thus get to know their pupils and be known by them. The environment is simply less daunting than that of secondary school.

In secondary schools, however, the problems become acute. Adolescents form and need strong friendships, from which a Down's Syndrome girl, for example, who may have been an amiable enough companion when she was younger, will now be excluded; her contemporaries having grown out of her reach. The obsessive eccentricities of the Asperger's boy will no longer be tolerated and he will be bullied and teased, or at best simply neglected. There is a body of evidence to suggest that this is happening. Again, the increasingly disciplined work expected from students who are to be successful at secondary school may be more easily disrupted by those who, because they are floundering and failing, may fall back on noisy or violent behaviour or perhaps stop attending school altogether. Disruptive pupils, even if few in number, adversely affect the learning of the rest; yet it is often hard to prove that this is so. If it cannot be proved, and if the parents still express a wish that their disruptive child attend a mainstream school, then since the Special Educational Needs and Disability Act 2002 the headteacher and governors may be liable to a criminal charge if they refuse to allow him to attend the school.

In 2004 the government published a White Paper entitled 'Removing Barriers to Achievement' as an answer to two highly critical reports by the Audit Commission, released in 2002, on the efficacy of the current provision for children with special educational needs. The first of these was entitled 'Statutory Assessment and Statements: In Need of Review?' The second was 'Special Educational Needs: A Mainstream Issue'. In the introduction to the White Paper, four main points made by the Audit Commission were listed: that too many children waited too long for provision; that children are turned away from mainstream schools, despite the fact that, since 2001, they are entitled to attend them if their parents so wish; that special schools are uncertain of their role; and that there is too much variation between different Local Authorities in the matter of provision. The Audit Commission was indeed critical of these faults in the system. But they went much further: they suggested that the present framework of provision, including the issuing of statements for some, but not all, children with special needs, was irretrievably bureaucratic, and had possibly outlived its usefulness. This suggestion, discussed in some detail in the first of the Audit Commission's papers and referred to again in the second, was not considered at all in the White Paper.

During the course of a debate in the House of Lords on 29 January 2003, triggered by the Audit Commission Report, ministers and backbenchers repeatedly referred to the statement of special educational need as a 'safety net' which must stay in place at all costs, however expensive and bureaucratic the system had become. The question of statements was not seen to have any connection with the policy of inclusion. Statemented children must still, in the vast majority of cases, be educated alongside their contemporaries in mainstream schools. This remained the overriding consideration; and there was, according to ministers, no need to take a new look at the system of provision. But they failed to ask what *purpose* statements actually served, or whether mainstream school was always an environment within which needy children, with or without statements, could reasonably be expected to learn.

In October 2004 Ofsted published a paper no less critical of current provision than those of the Audit Commission (Ofsted, 2004). They found that the government's framework of inclusion had had little effect on the number of pupils with special needs properly catered for in mainstream schools, and that the number of pupils sent to referral units outside the school, or to independent special schools had actually risen. Moreover schools were finding it increasingly difficult to manage pupils with social and behavioural difficulties. Even where students with special needs and sometimes statements were admitted and retained in schools, too often the price of this was that they were taught almost entirely by teaching assistants who were not fully qualified, and therefore they did not benefit from the best teaching. This was, of course, especially true in secondary schools, where it was noted also that 'behaviour was often disruptive and sometimes very poor. Attendance was often unsatisfactory. Decisions on pupil grouping were sometimes evidently based on a desire to protect more able pupils from disruption' (Ofsted 2004: page 17). Many teachers had not been trained to deal with these difficulties, and turnover was often high, thus adding to the problems experienced by the pupils.

The policy of issuing statements of special educational need for certain pupils, while it may ensure for some a place at a special school, seems to have had little or no effect on those children who remain at maintained schools. In the case of such pupils, there is no evidence that the statement serves as a 'safety net'. If the issuing of a statement for a child were to be used as a passport to an appropriate special school there would be some purpose to be served by it. But this, of course, would be contrary to the policy of inclusion. It is time now to consider that policy itself.

3. The ideal of inclusion reconsidered

The concept of inclusion springs from hearts in the right place. Its meaning, however, is far from clear, and in practice it often means that children are physically included but emotionally excluded. I argue that schools should not be seen as microcosms of society, and that the tendency of children to bully those they see as different should be addressed, in part, by the creation of small schools. Inclusion should mean being involved in a common enterprise of learning, rather than being necessarily under the same roof.

A central argument of this paper is that government should rethink its framework of inclusion. It may not be easy to persuade them to do this. Inclusion is a fundamental concept in their thinking not only about schools but more widely about leisure activities, about employment, about higher education and the arts. It is linked to the ideas of 'accessibility' and 'widening participation'.

In the context of the arts, for example, inclusiveness dictates that no art form should be encouraged, let alone subsidized, that is not popular, already demanded by the public or enjoyed by a majority.

The idea that there may be experts in the arts who have better and more discriminating judgment than others less knowledgeable or experienced than they, and who may open the eyes of the public to pleasures they have not yet experienced, is held to be elitist. In the world of leisure activities, inclusiveness entails that if guided walks in the Lake District, for example, are not wanted by everyone, including disadvantaged people of various kinds (and heaven knows what would happen if everyone did want them), then they should no longer be provided.

In the context of education, we need to ask whether children who have special needs, that is children who for various reasons have difficulties in learning at school, do in fact participate more in the enterprise of education if they are taught in mainstream schools than if they are taught in special schools. The answer, surely, is that some of them do, but some of them do not. As I have suggested already, 'SEN children' increasingly tend to be lumped together indiscriminately, as though they share in common a right to be educated in mainstream schools. But the idea of 'learner-centred education', increasingly seen as important for educational success, should remind us that for some children participation is impossible in the context of the mainstream school.

One cannot hope to eliminate such a widespread and heterogeneous vision of the good as the vision of inclusion, or 'one society'. And of course it springs from hearts in the right place: a commitment to equality of opportunity. But school is not a microcosm of society. Schools are for children, not adults; and children still need help in their development. Education is a unique enterprise in that it is necessarily a temporary phase of life, directed towards the future, towards life after school. The pursuit of equality at school may mean taking whatever steps are necessary now to ensure equal opportunities later on. It should not be thought to entail an insistence that all children within a given area should be literally in the same school. What is needed is that all children should be included within a common educational project, not that they should be included under one roof.

I would like to invite ministers to consider a definition of inclusion suggested by the National Association of Head Teachers in their 'Policy Paper on Special Schools', published in July 2003. They write:

> Inclusion is a process that maximizes the entitlement of all pupils to a broad, relevant and stimulating curriculum, which is delivered in the environment that will have the greatest impact on their learning. All schools, whether special or mainstream, should reflect a culture in which the institution adapts to meet the needs of its pupils and is provided with the resources to enable this to happen. (page 1)

They gloss this definition as follows:

> Inclusive schooling is essential to the development of an inclusive society. It involves having an education service that ensures that provision and funding is there to enable pupils to be educated in the most appropriate setting. This will be the one in which they can be most fully included in the life of their school community and which gives them a sense both of belonging and achieving. (page 1)

The last sentence is the one to which ministers should pay the most attention. Inclusion is not a matter of where you are geographically, but of where you feel you belong. There are many children, and especially adolescents, identified as having special educational needs, who can never feel that they belong in a large mainstream school.

One of crucial changes must therefore be that the concept of special educational needs is broken down. We must give up the idea that SEN is the name of a unified class of students at whom, in a uniform way, the policy of inclusion can be directed. That schools should as far as possible adapt their premises to make all parts of them more accessible to children in wheelchairs, or whose mobility is otherwise restricted is something that, though it may be expensive, is a policy that is easy to understand and in principle possible to implement. Special equipment may make it possible that some children with sensory deprivation or who cannot write or communicate without electronic aids can be taught in the ordinary classroom. Schools could, and in my view should, return to having full-time school nurses, so that children who need medication, or who are, say, prone to epileptic fits or severe attacks of asthma might safely be educated there.

However not every child who suffers from such disabilities as these will flourish in a mainstream school, however much the environment is adapted. Children with such disabilities are often vulnerable in other ways as well. And even more importantly, there is the large number of children (the largest among the SEN) who for emotional, behavioural or more strictly cognitive reasons (or a combination of these) are genuinely unable to learn in a regular classroom, and who distract other children from learning if they are placed there. For these, the concept of inclusion is often stretched so that they are deemed to be included even if they attend classes in a special unit on the campus of the main school. But life on the school bus or in the school grounds may still be traumatic for them. Among children for whom mainstream school may be inappropriate is the growing number diagnosed as suffering from autism, at some point along the autistic spectrum. For this large group of children it is essential that we raise the question what their 'inclusion' in mainstream school amounts to, and whether it is experienced by them as a good. The reality seems to be, in many cases, that it is experienced as a painful kind of exclusion.

It is especially in considering these children that governments must come to recognize that, even if inclusion is an ideal for society in general, it may not always be an ideal for school. For schools, as I said, are not microcosms of society. They are full of people who are as yet immature, who cannot be expected to know how to behave until they are taught, and who are even more prone to persecute the weak and gang up against the eccentric than are people in the world outside. At the same time, it is characteristic of schools that their life is highly structured and lived at a great pace; it is also lived in public. Far less than in the outside world is it possible for a child who is seen as 'different' to find anywhere to hide or to avoid the bewildering demands that are made on him, or the jokes of which he is the butt and which he cannot understand, still less find funny. At school such a pupil may be intensely vulnerable. He may be a fragile individual whom we have a duty both to protect and to support.

I shall return to the question of what needs to be done to supply such protection and support. But first I must anticipate an objection to my thesis that inclusion in mainstream schools may not always be a good. It is sometimes argued that inclusion is a human right, and the Disability Discrimination Act did no more than recognize that fact. And because inclusion is a human right it is self-evidently a good. That it seems not always to work, or often to produce results that are harmful is irrelevant. If something is self-evidently good, there is no point in seeking empirical evidence of its value. To pursue it constitutes an imperative. Schools must make it work.

My reply to this is implicit in what I have already said. What is a manifest good in society, and what it is my right to have, namely access to all the advantages that membership of society may bring, may not be what is best for me as a schoolchild. The original idea of special needs entails that children are not alike in all respects: some are more vulnerable than others, and need more protection from the rest if they are to be able to learn. It is their right to learn that we must defend, not their right to learn in the same environment as everyone else. For them we must emphasize their differences (i.e. their needs) as learners, not their similarities with all the rest. Whatever may be the merits of deploying the rhetoric of human rights in the demand for inclusion for the disabled in society as a whole, it cannot be argued a priori that values within a school must be identical to values in the society of adults. And this rhetoric in the context of schoolchildren may lead to insensitivity to their needs as well as a culpable disregard for evidence of how children can flourish educationally and what factors may prevent their flourishing. Children, even more than adults, need to believe that they are valued. They need to feel that there is a society, even (or indeed especially) a small one, where they are at home. This is particularly true of children who, as they grow older, come to realize painfully that they are 'different', and that, for whatever reason, they cannot fit in with the norm. For such child the inevitable toughness required for survival in a large busy school is an impossible goal.

The National Autistic Society has found that many more children with Autistic Spectrum Disorders are excluded from school than the average (21 per cent versus 1.2 per cent), and that among autistic children with high ability this figure rises to 29 per cent. The psychiatrist Lorna Wing has told me that in her clinical work she has met able autistic adults who carry the misery of their mainstream school days with them into adult life, sometimes with disastrous consequences. The fact is that, if educated in mainstream schools, many such children are not included at all. They suffer all the pains of the permanent outsider. No political ideology should impose this on them.

I have already remarked that we must break down the concept of SEN in a proper analytic spirit, and acknowledge rather than blur genuine differences. We must not assume that all special needs are the same, still less that that mainstream schooling is best for all children with such needs. There are some hopeful signs that government is beginning to be open to innovative ideas. The concentration of resources on the early years of childhood and the support of Sure Start is one such sign. For there is much evidence to show that nursery education improves a child's educational chances permanently. And with improved ability to learn there goes improved behaviour. Thus more widespread and more professional nursery education ought to go a long way towards reducing the largest category of children manifesting special needs later in their school career. For these children the question of inclusion would no longer arise; they would already be securely included. Such initiatives should not be confined to inner cities or to areas of perceived deprivation. Poverty and deprivation exist in small towns as well as large, in rural as well as urban areas. Investment in Sure Start will pay enormous dividends later. Again, nurture groups within primary schools, where children with social, emotional and behavioural difficulties are taught in small informal groups by specially trained teachers, sometimes for as long as two years, before being fully returned to the classroom, are shown by the research that the Nurture Group Network is carrying out to be remarkably effective in enabling children to overcome their difficulties and to be eager for and receptive of learning as their school career goes on. These initiatives show how beneficial it has been surreptitiously and without repealing the 1981 Act to allow that children from deprived backgrounds have special educational needs, particularly in the matter of communication and conversation. Many such children, whether English is their first language or not, start school with virtually no vocabulary, and no understanding of how to do things with other children, including singing with them, dancing with them and playing games.

Yet despite the now proven benefits of early intervention, there will remain children for whom mainstream schools will not work. To its credit, the government has recognized the need to deploy the expertise of teachers in special schools to support and soon, I hope, to train teachers in mainstream schools, who have the task of identifying and providing for children with special educational needs. This was something that was recommended as long ago as 1978, when the report of the Government Inquiry was published, but until now, no government has done more than offer it a ritual nod. Now it has been announced that 12 schools will be designated specialist schools in SEN, and teachers from these schools will have as part of their duties to go round to mainstream schools to support the teachers there, and offer the benefit of their expertise. Even more significantly, the 12 schools have been divided into four different specialities: communication and interaction (perhaps for autistic children); cognition and learning; behavioural, emotional and social difficulties; and sensory and physical needs. This reflects a very welcome recognition that SEN is not one phenomenon, but many. Excellent though this initiative is, it will not directly or immediately benefit any child with special needs unless he is fortunate enough to live within or not far outside the catchment area of one of these specialist schools that happens to fit with his particular disability.

Nevertheless, it is huge step forward, if only for the rather absurd reason that, while the designation 'special school' has always alarmed parents, and made them anxious to avoid sending their children to one if avoidance were possible, the designation 'specialist school' sounds better, and indeed commands a certain amount of respect among parents, at least in large cities, where one may actually choose to send one's child to a specialist school (in, say, languages) rather than to another available school.

There is another even more optimistic trend. There are some schools, (and I am directly acquainted with only one, Marshfields School in Peterborough, but there are more than 20 others), which are both special schools, and also specialist schools, specializing in this case, and probably in most of the others, in IT. This is a school for pupils with moderate learning difficulties. All of them have statements, and will not be admitted to the school without one. Having been a regular special school since 1971, in 2003 it became a specialist technology college, which meant that it had extra funding, and could offer specialist IT teaching not only for its own students but for others who might come either in the evenings after school, or when they had left school, and wanted to acquire new skills or qualifications. Inclusion is thus ensured; but it is students from outside who are 'included' within the community of pupils with statements of special educational need. Those pupils of Marshfields who stay on at school after the age of 16 (and many do) have a choice of courses, either entirely within the school, or a joint course with the local college of further education. The employment prospects of pupils from the school are excellent. But, more important, the school is highly respected by parents, and is an object of deep commitment and loyalty to its pupils, many of whom prefer to stay at the school rather than return to mainstream schools, though ready to do so. The relation between the pupils and the teachers is excellent, and there is, apparently, hardly any bullying. This successful special school seems to me to be a model that could well be followed by others, once it has been acknowledged that special schools have a role, not just for the most profoundly disabled, but for many other children who will eventually take their place as competent and responsible members of society.

So successful is this school that it has repeatedly been asked to expand. At present its pupils number about 156; and the head and governors have refused all invitations to exceed that number. In this I believe they are right. It seems to me that one of the main defects in the present educational system is the size of schools. I cannot understand why government proudly says that a successful secondary school will be given permission to expand and increase its numbers. It never seems to have struck ministers that perhaps a key to the success of schools that do succeed is that they are not too big; and that if they became bigger there is no guarantee that their success would continue. Their character and ethos might radically change. I believe that the single most effective way to improve educational provision, especially for the fragile children I have already identified, and for others who suffer from learning disabilities, is to provide small maintained schools to which students could have access if, and only if, they had a statement. Statements should indeed be used as passports to such schools, and for no other purpose, so there would be no pupils with statements in mainstream schools. Some of the pupils in mainstream schools would of course have special needs, but only such as could be met within the normal resources of the school and for the most part in the normal classroom. If their needs were more acute, and they were still failing at school, or behaving disruptively or truanting, they should be given a statement, an entry pass to a small school. In this way parents would come to regard it as a privilege for their child to have access to such a special, or specialist, school. They would be anxious for their children to get in, as parents are for their children to get in to Marshfields. For in a small school there is the possibility of real, experienced inclusion. Pupils know and are known to their teachers. Teachers are accessible to pupils who are encouraged to talk to them. There is a far lower turnover of staff, even where the school takes pupils with severe behavioural problems. Pupils can identify with and take pride in their school. Classes are small, and if someone is taken out for extra help this is not equivalent to being relegated to a special unit, only loosely attached to the main school.

Another group of children for whom I believe that small schools are essential is that of children in care, so called 'looked after' children. It is at last beginning to be recognized that the education of these children is a disgrace. In the 1970s there were still children's homes where education was supposed to be provided on the premises, but the teachers were employees not of the Local Education Authority but of the Social Services Department, and they were subject to no form of inspection. Education was at the very bottom of the list of priorities for such homes. Those days have passed. But it is still true that about 20 per cent more children in care are excluded from mainstream schools than children who live with their families, and the truanting rate is equally high. Here is a group of children suffering extreme emotional deprivation, and hence in urgent need of the kind of education to be provided only in the properly inclusive environment of the small school, where they may begin to see that there are adults who value them and their abilities, whether these are low or high, who have hope for them, and actually want them to succeed. We now know and are allowed to acknowledge that the kind of social deprivation experienced by such children brings with it special educational needs. These can be met only by an educational environment within which they can learn to feel that they are valued, and so can learn to value what they are offered.

Small schools are, of course, expensive. But they need not offer such a wide range of subjects as a large comprehensive school. Many pupils might be ready to move back to a mainstream school by the end of Year 11, or to leave school for an apprenticeship. But in any case the money would be well spent, if it saved children from exclusion, truanting and the long-term social consequences that these bring.

Small schools (specialist schools, special schools, whatever they are called) should be linked with statements. This would get rid of the anomaly that within the same school and the same class there may be some pupils with statements and some without them whose needs nevertheless appear to be much the same. My hope would be that gradually parents (and employers) would stop thinking automatically that if someone has been to a special school he is doomed. If the attitude of parents to special schools could change, this might to some extent reduce the confrontation and ill-feeling that the present system generates, as well as saving some of the money currently wasted on tribunals and appeals. No parent would ask for a statement for their child unless they were convinced that they would prefer the child to go to a different school. And wherever possible the child himself should have his wishes taken into account.

I must add that ministers and civil servants cannot escape blame for the low esteem in which special schools are currently held. Their treatment of such schools as regrettable necessities, suitable only for the most severely disabled, has to a considerable extent made this outcome inevitable.

There are now some hopeful signs, but it would be wrong to be too optimistic. I believe that the reforms advocated by Tomlinson should have been implemented and put in place as soon as possible. Nothing would go further towards ensuring the proper inclusion of all children within one educational enterprise than the introduction of one overarching system of diplomas with varied content, and the end of segregation between A level students and the rest. Moreover the kind of school where pupils did not necessarily study all their subjects with their own year-group, but could go at their own pace, taking grades whether in academic or in vocational subjects as they were ready for them, would itself have served to bring about a properly inclusive school. This would have provided the kind of achievable goals for the less academic that might have motivated them to stay at school, and have given them a new sense of their own worth. Here sadly was a missed opportunity to increase inclusiveness in a realistic way. I am appalled to think that the government, committed as it is to the rhetoric of inclusion, is so conservative and timid in its thinking that it cannot even now contemplate abandoning the divisive and increasingly useless so-called gold standard of A levels. Such conservatism is as thoughtless and wrong-headed as the obstinate adherence to statements as a safety net.

Besides the low achievers, there is another group of pupils for whom Tomlinson's flexibility, his system within which the needs of the learner are firmly at the centre, would have been highly beneficial. This is the group who are known as 'gifted'. The chance to work towards elements of each of the four grades of diploma at the student's own pace (rather as Associated Board Music examinations are carefully graded in difficulty, but with no age restrictions attached to any grade) would mean that those who were outstandingly talented in, say, mathematics could advance swiftly to the study of mathematics outside school, at a college or university, while remaining at school for other subjects as well as for social life and sport. Mathematically gifted children undoubtedly have special needs; they can advance with a speed that is incomprehensible to other children, and if they have no opportunity to do so they may become bored and disaffected. Again, it has long been recognized that gifted musicians have special needs, including opportunities in their timetables for practice and performance. The same is true of gifted students of dance. Government has recognized this up to a point in its policy of grants to enable such children to attend fee-paying specialist schools, such as the Purcell School. But there are many 'gifted' children who do not receive grants, and the introduction of the Tomlinson reforms would have gone a long way towards meeting their needs. It is to be hoped that such reforms will be reconsidered in the near future.

4. Conclusions

Section 3 contained my own thoughts about possible ways forward. It in no way stands as a fully reasoned set of recommendations. For no serious suggestions for reform can be made without proper research and a proper reliance on evidence. This is why I regard it as essential that there should be a government-funded independent Committee of Inquiry into the current state of special education, empowered to make recommendations based on the evidence of experts, especially teachers. This is my only firm conclusion.

That conclusion apart, I am convinced of two things. First, the present system of the statement of needs, however lovingly ministers cling to it (as lovingly, indeed, as they cling to A levels), must be reexamined and put to a different use if it cannot be abolished. This is necessary for many reasons, but one is enough: it is wasteful and bureaucratic, and causes bad blood between parents and Local Authorities and schools.

Second, the idea of inclusion should be rethought insofar at least as it applies to education at school. If it is too much to hope that it will be demoted from its present position at the top of the list of educational values, then at least let it be redefined so that it allows children to pursue the common goals of education in the environment within which they can best be taught and learn.

Finally, with our growing recognition of the crucial difference that social differences make to educational chances, we must invent a new kind of specialist school that can cater properly not only for children with specific disabilities which render them unable to function in large schools, but also for children with needs that arise from social disadvantage. Of particular concern are children in care, who often need an environment within which they can be known and supported by their teachers, so that relationships of trust may develop. It is my strong conviction that these must be small schools. But what is needed is hard evidence to support this view. One person's conviction is not enough.

Note

1   This chapter is a reproduction of Warnock's original 2005 pamphlet, second edition, published by the Society of Philosophy of Education of Great Britain.

References

Audit Commission (2002), 'Statutory Assessment and Statements: in Need of Review?'. London: Audit Commission, www.dfes.gov.uk.

Audit Commission (2002), 'Special Educational Needs: A Mainstream Issue'. London: Audit Commission.

Department of Education and Science (1978), *Special Educational Needs* (The Warnock Report), London: HMSO.

Department for Education (1994), *Code of Practice on the Identification and Assessment of Special Educational Needs,* London: HMSO.

Department for Education and Skills (2001), 'Inclusive Schooling: Children with Special Educational Needs' London: DfES,www.dfes.gov.uk.

Department for Education and Skills (2004) *Removing Barriers to Achievement: The Government's Strategy for SEN* (White Paper), London: DfES, www.teachernet.gov.uk/wholeschool/sen/senstrategy/.

Dyson A (2001), 'Special Needs in the Twenty-first Century: Where We've Been and Where We're Going', *British Journal of Special Education*, vol. 28, no.1, 24–29

National Association of Head Teachers (2003), 'Policy Paper on Special Schools' www.naht.org.uk.

Ofsted (2004) 'Special Educational Needs and Disability: Towards Inclusive Schools'. London: Audit Commission, www.ofsted.gov.uk/publications/index.

A Response to 'Special Educational Needs: A New Look'

Brahm Norwich

Introduction

Mary Warnock's pamphlet was written and published in 2005 and now, some years later, much has happened in special educational needs policy, partly in response to the pamphlet. So, in my response to the pamphlet, I will organize my comments into three parts, following this introduction. In the first part, I will outline various responses to it. Informal comments were expressed through verbal exchanges in professional settings and in the media and through letters, articles and books. Formal responses have been represented by the House of Commons' Reports, including the setting up of the Lamb Inquiry and the current Ofsted examination of special educational needs. In the second part, I will examine the key positions and arguments expressed in Mary Warnock's pamphlet. This will then lead to the third and final part of my response, which will set out some personal positions and arguments relevant to some of the key points that she raises about policy and practice in this field, in particular the status of the concept of special educational needs, the role of statements and the future of inclusion.

1. Immediate responses to the pamphlet

As expected, responses to the Warnock pamphlet reflected varied and conflicting policy and political stances to inclusion. Correspondence and articles in *The Times Educational Supplement* (TES) can be seen as representative of some of these views. For example, Mark Vaughn from the Centre for Studies of Inclusive Education, in an article on 17 June 2005 criticized the pamphlet as being 'rooted in the past'. He claimed that Mary Warnock had 'missed out on 20 years of global debate and development of effective practice that put inclusion of disabled students on a human rights stage'. He pointed to her reference to inclusion as a 'disastrous legacy' as evidence of her ignoring the many examples of inclusion working well and explained how she had failed to understand that 'segregation is and always has been a form of discrimination'. Her attitude, according to him, was offensive to professionals and insulting to disabled children and families. His defence of inclusive practice included admitting some 'bad inclusive practice', which he put in the context of some 'bad education' generally. Had Mary Warnock spent some of the last 20 years talking to disabled adults who describe themselves as 'special-school survivors', she might, according to him, have been a supporter of the social model of disability. What is interesting about Mark Vaughn's response is not so much the personalizing of the argument – the attributed experiences of offence and insult and the advice to find out more – but his point that the original Warnock Report had never been in favour of a fully inclusive education. The Warnock Report and the legislative framework established in 1981 did recognize the continuing requirement for some separate provision in the form of special units or special schools. So, the 2005 pamphlet was not as radical a change in Mary Warnock's position as some superficial commentaries have noted. Her 2005 pamphlet can be interpreted rather as representing her concerns with the balance between special and mainstream school placements for children and young people with significant special educational needs.

Mark Vaughn's position was criticized in the TES (1 July 2005) by Rona Tutt, past president of the National Association of Head Teachers (NAHT), who defended the Warnock pamphlet by asserting that Mary Warnock had continued her interest in the field since 1978. It was Mark Vaughn, she argued, who was 'attempting to halt progress with his continued use of the term "segregation" and his talk of "special-school survivors"'. Rhona Tutt argued for a concept of an inclusive school service which consists of special and mainstream schools and reminded us that 'the main political parties and teaching unions have all expressed the need to maintain a range of provision, so that all pupils have a chance of receiving an education appropriate to their needs'.

Another relevant position from someone who described himself as 'a young turk for integration', Colin Low, writing in the TES (17 February 2006) as chairman of the Royal National Institute for the Blind (RNIB), sets the debate in a historical context that the original campaign and movement were about there being a *choice* of a mainstream school option for disabled children and young people. Colin Low presents the argument for inclusion as having been won, in that 'inclusion is now the placement of choice'. He comes to Mary Warnock's defence by suggesting that the annoyance of inclusion supporters with her 2005 pamphlet was because it 'will halt the steady progress to full inclusion of all disabled children in mainstream schools'. He also suggested that it is the pro-inclusion lobby that is 'forcing the issue by pressing for abolition of special schools'. However, he was clear in his support for the mainstream school 'being progressively geared up to meet' more of the needs of disabled children and young people.

These written exchanges show the main terms in which the debates have taken place since the 2005 pamphlet by some key actors in the field. These issues revolve around the extent to which mainstream schools can and should accommodate the needs of all children and young people (sometimes called 'full inclusion') and therefore whether there will be separate provision in special schools. Though Colin Low presents his position on a future for special schools in terms of it being an option for parental choice, the current legislative commitment to mainstream placements is not only in terms of parental preference. It is also about whether mainstream placement negatively affects the education of other children. This condition might conflict with parental preference, so the extent of provision for children with significant and complex special educational needs in mainstream schools goes beyond choice principles. Rhona Tutt and Colin Low, despite their other differences, represent the position about inclusion and special schools that sees a continuing role for special schools by contrast with Mark Vaughn's position for the closure of all special schools. However, while Tutt's position is more aligned with Mary Warnock's 2005 pamphlet, Low's position is clearly in favour of reducing special schools as much as possible. Comparing these three positions with Mary Warnock's in the 2005 pamphlet suggests three versions:

1. Special schools to increase slightly – Warnock position
2. Special schools to reduce as mainstream becomes more accommodating – Low's position
3. Special schools to close in foreseeable future – Vaughn's position

These different views about the future of inclusion and special schools were not the only matters that were considered in the House of Commons Select Committee Report on Special Educational Needs

(House of Commons Education and Skills Committee, 2006). This Report also dealt with the wider issues in the field and in particular the role of statements in the system. However, that the Select Committee took up the issues about education provision for pupils with special educational needs can be attributed partly to the impact of Mary Warnock's 2005 pamphlet. The Committee's Report refers to her pamphlet at key points in their setting the scene for the inquiry.

Select Committee's position

The Select Committee Report started by acknowledging the scale of special educational needs – about 1.5 million pupils so identified, about 3 per cent with statements and about 1 per cent in special schools. It also recognizes that 'many children are receiving the education they need in an appropriate setting. But, this is countered by the claim that there are 'difficulties faced by a large number of parents for whom the system is failing to meet the needs of their children'. However, the balance between the former positive aspects and the latter negative aspects is something that remained uncertain in their Report.

The impact of Mary Warnock's arguments about the confusion over inclusion policy on the Committee's approach is also evident in their Report. Where the Committee's Report goes beyond the 2005 pamphlet is to hold the government to account for its policy position. The Report reveals the contradictory perspective of the then Parliamentary Under-Secretary, Lord Adonis, and the recent Government Strategy about inclusion and special schools. Adonis told the inquiry that the government did not have a policy of inclusion that resulted in closing special schools and that there was no official view about what proportion of pupils should be in special schools. Yet, as the Report pointed out, the 2004 Government Strategy (the 10-year strategy 'Removing Barriers to Achievement') stated that 'the proportion of children educated in special schools should fall over time' (DfES, page 37). The Committee went further to argue that, based on its 2004 Strategy and other statutory and non-statutory guidance, it was reasonable for those involved in SEN to assume that the government holds a policy of inclusion that involves a reduction in special school numbers and a reduced reliance on statements.

The government presented a position to the inquiry that it had no policy to close special schools, that special schools had an important role within the overall pattern of provision and that their position was one of a 'flexible continuum of provision'. The Select Committee's response to this was that more consistency between this 'flexible continuum' position and previous guidance and approaches was needed. This inconsistency led the Committee to call for national strategic direction and the need for a 'major public review of SEN policy' (section 31). Part of the Committee's call for greater clarification of inclusion policy was the need to pull together disability and SEN agendas and legislation. It noted that SEN legislation was about 'meeting needs', while disability discrimination was about making 'reasonable adjustments'. The Committee also focused on the 'inbuilt conflict of interest' (section 26) that existed with the Local Authority having the duty to both assess needs and arrange provision to meet these needs, within limited resources. It recommended that this link between assessment and funding be broken, a recommendation which the Committee came back to in its second brief report on SEN (to be discussed further below).

The Select Committee, following the lead of the Audit Commission Report (2002) and the Ofsted Report (2004), among other sources, as well as Warnock's 2005 pamphlet, concluded that there were 'serious flaws' in the SEN system as regards:

> standards and consistency of provision, the statementing process, fair access to schools and outcomes for children and young people with SEN and disabilities (section 141).

Special reference was made to the 'unhappiness felt by some parents' with the statementing process and the battles that some parents had to fight to secure what they considered to be appropriate provision for their children. The Committee recognized that seeking a reduction of statements not only depends on improving the skills and capacity of mainstream schools, but requires a system with 'much greater clarification and much stronger guidance on minimum standards of provision' (section 153). What was required, according to the Report, was a 'national framework with local flexibility' and that part of this clarification would be national guidance on when to issue statements.

Though it held back from making specific recommendations about alternative models to the current statementing one, it drew attention to the new Scottish model of 'additional support needs' as evidence that reform to the 1981 legislative system is possible. It was concluded that the government had responsibility for designing a better system; one that also involved 'early identification and intervention, efficient and equitable resource allocation and appropriate placement of pupils based on their needs and taking account of parental preferences' (section 163).

The Committee also concluded that parental choice was not always being upheld by Local Authorities, whether for a special school or a mainstream placement with 'reasonable adjustments'. In this respect the Committee advocated a system of provision where there is a 'broad range of high quality, well resourced, flexible provision to meet the needs of all children' (section 171). This meant that Local Authorities would have a range of 'specialist' and 'mainstream' provision for the range of pupils with SEN and disabilities, to which parents would have an entitlement, as set out in a statutory guidance framework that would be monitored regularly (sections 267–8).

The Committee also had clear recommendations about 'equipping the workforce' as regards provision for pupils with SEN/disabilities. Nothing less than SEN training as a core and compulsory part of initial teacher training/education was acceptable to the Committee. Here they referred to the three-fold strategy for SEN training, initial training, as newly qualified teachers and in continuing professional development as well as the three-stage 'training triangle' model from the 2004 Government SEN Strategy:

1. Core skills for all teachers/all schools
2. Advanced skills for some teachers/ all schools
3. Specialist skills in some schools

Connected to training as a top priority were recommendations about the role of SEN coordinators as qualified and appropriately trained teachers in all schools in a senior management position. There were also other recommendations made by the Select Committee about specialist support services, the role of educational psychologists, the place of early intervention and managing key transitions, including post-16 transitions, partnership work and the Every Child Matters agenda and parent partnerships.

Government's response to Select Committee Report

The government's response to the Committee's Report was to accept some recommendations but to reject the thrust of the Report and other key recommendations. The main argument was that there were no grounds for a fundamental review of the SEN system. This was based on assertions about the progress made in implementing the 2004 Strategy, the rising spending on the field, the high proportion of statements completed on time and the Ofsted 2006 survey which was taken to indicate some improvements in SEN provision (Ofsted, 2006).

The main reason given for not having a major review was about the uncertainty that this would cause which would, it was argued, distract from making further progress. The government also rejected the key recommendation about changing the system of statutory assessment and statementing. The reasons were confined to assertions that more statements were completed on time and that government SEN advisers had recently reported on improved communications between Local Authorities and parents over statutory assessments. Nor was the government impressed with suggestions for removing statutory assessment from Local Authorities. This defence of the current system included reference to Local Authorities assuming a more strategic role and the new duties under the Disability Discrimination legislation of 2005. In this way the government opposed radical change in favour of an approach that built further capacity in the workforce, improved the range of provision for diverse needs, secured better coordination and commissioning of services as well as improved accountability for the progress and outcomes that children achieve.

Generalities like these were also evident in the response to the Select Committee's key recommendation of a national framework with local flexibility. This time the government sidestepped the recommendation by acknowledging that this was desirable, but was in fact being built through the Every Child Matters change programme. This programme, it was suggested, provides for integrated planning, joint commissioning of services, partnership in service delivery and accountability for service quality and their impact on outcomes. In conclusion the government's response identified five key areas for action over the next few years:

1. Building capacity in workforce
2. Promoting a flexible continuum of local provision
3. Improving accountability for outcomes achieved by children
4. Strengthening of parent partnerships
5. Improved provision for children with behaviour, emotional and social difficulties as well as those with autistic difficulties

It is interesting that when the press release about the government's response was issued in October 2006, it focused mainly on what has probably been the one area of the five above which was new, the moves to strengthen teaching in special educational needs in schools. Recently, the Training and Development Agency (TDA) has developed SEN and disability units for primary undergraduate teacher training courses. These were to be followed by units for secondary and PGCE courses in 2009. The government is also developing the skills of the early years and schools workforce through the Inclusion

Development Programme and promoting specialist training through the work of three Trusts dealing with communication, autism and dyslexia.

More recent developments

As part of the government's response to the Select Committee Report, it requested that Ofsted review progress in relation to the above five key priority areas in 2009–10. The aim is to have this review address the question of whether the present SEN framework needs fundamental change. However, the Select Committee was dissatisfied with the government's response and found a specific topic on which they could come back to hold a second smaller scale inquiry: the previous recommendation that the assessment of need be separated from the funding of provision. The Committee was looking for a series of options which would enable this separation without having an assessment quango, as the government suggested in their response. When the Select Committee reported in October 2007, it concluded that assessment could be separated from funding and expected a government response to these options and some wider issues they raised. The three options were:

1. Assessment of need commissioned by Local Authorities: this was seen as the most practical way to achieve separation of provision/funding from assessment.
2. Delegating assessment to schools: this involved schools or groups of schools undertaking needs assessment.
3. Making educational psychology services more independent: this could be done by government guidance to authorities about having psychologists making unfettered assessments or by government funding psychological assessment directly.

The second Committee Report also raised questions for government about how the use of the Common Assessment Framework, which has been developed as part of the Every Child Matters developments (see more detail in third section, page 83), will affect assessment of special educational needs and statementing.

The most recent government response to this second Report was made in February 2008, when the government set up a group of expert advisers, under the chairmanship of Brian Lamb, the Chair of the Special Educational Consortium, to advise on the most effective ways of increasing parental confidence in the SEN assessment process. The Lamb Inquiry has been asked to:

1. Consider a range of ways in which parental confidence in the SEN assessment process might be increased
2. Commission and evaluate innovative projects in these areas
3. Draw on the evidence of other work currently commissioned by the Department
4. Take into account the evidence of the submissions to the two Select Committee Reports in 2006 and 2007

This Inquiry has already commissioned innovative projects to promote its aims and will report in September 2009 and according to the Government will be available to the Ofsted SEN survey of 2009/10 and help to inform national developments.[2]

2. A detailed examination of 'Special Education Needs: A New Look'

It is evident that Mary Warnock's pamphlet came at the beginning of a very active period of policy analysis and deliberation, and without doubt was instrumental in initiating this phase of review as well as influencing the terms in which it has been conducted. In this section I will examine specific aspects of the 'New Look' pamphlet.

Overview

Mary Warnock makes a clear statement of belief that 30 years after the Warnock Report it is time for a 'radical review'. It might be thought that this pamphlet represents a change of mind about the field, as some have suggested, but there is no evidence for this. In the preface to a 1993 book *Special Education in Britain after Warnock* (Visser and Upton, 1993), she argued that, in the light of the Education Reform Act 1988, with its introduction of the National Curriculum and local management of schools, and other legislation, the 1981 Act – which derived from the 1978 Warnock Report – was then 'out-of-date' (page ix). Drawing on the arguments and evidence from an earlier Audit Commission report (Audit Commission, 1992) she concluded that the issuing of statements had 'fallen into disarray'. She lamented the growth of litigation in the relationships between parents and Local Authorities, especially in the times of financial hardship as applied in the early 1990s, when statements were seen as one way of binding the Local Authority to provide. She identified growing adversarial attitudes, damaging trust, proving to be expensive and not benefiting anyone, except lawyers. She asserted that 'statementing ought to be abolished' (page ix). Though she did not comment on inclusion in this preface – the term itself had not been used at that time –she did show some of her critical attitudes to a social perspective on special educational needs that considered SEN to be a social construction or what she called a 'manipulative perception' of those who have 'no identifiable needs'. This perspective foreshadowed her later critiques in her 2005 pamphlet, to be discussed later.

In her 2005 overview Warnock also focuses initially on the central role of statements of special educational needs and again recognizes that they have been seriously criticized. She questions whether they provide a 'safety net' and should be retained for that reason. It is from the lack of clarity about the nature and purpose of statements that she identifies two concepts underlying this lack of clarity: the concept of 'special educational need' and the concept of 'inclusion'.

The pamphlet then examines these concepts by explaining that the SEN concept was introduced as an inclusive term to make a break from the medical assumption that children could be differentiated neatly into those who were normal and others who were handicapped. The significance of the word 'educational' in SEN was to highlight that needs were related to common educational goals to which all children would progress. However, progress towards these goals would vary, with varying degrees of difficulties along the way and with some requiring help. The role of statements, she explains, was to give rights to special provision and so confer responsibilities on Local Authorities to provide it. The problem, however, was that criteria for deciding when a statement of SEN was needed were not specified. While a child with a severe disability may be said, she argues, to need special help, this was less clear cut for children with milder difficulties or disabilities. She then states:

> The lack of clarity was reflected in the fact that our original guess of how many children would receive statements was wildly off the mark. We thought the figure would be around 2 per cent. The actual figure was around 20 per cent.

This position seems to imply that 20 per cent of pupils actually have had statements, but this has not been the case. The government statistics, quoted in the Select Committee Report, refer to the proportion of statements increasing through the 1990s to a peak of 3.1 per cent in 2001 and decreasing slightly to 2.9 per cent in 2005. There is a confusion here as it is clear that, while the 1978 Warnock Report did recognize that about one in five or 20 per cent of children might 'require special educational provision', the Report did not expect 20 per cent to have a statement. See these two quotes below to show this:

> In the light of the information available to us, including the estimate made by the Inner London Education Authority in 1971 after discussions with teachers, we estimate that up to one child in five is likely to require special educational provision at some point during his school career. (Warnock Report, 1978: section 3.17)

> We therefore recommend that a duty should be imposed on
> Authorities to maintain a record of children whom they judge to
> require special educational provision not normally available in the
> ordinary school, subject to the proviso that no child should be
> recorded without prior assessment by a multi-professional team.
> (Warnock Report, 1978: section 4.69)

The latter excerpt shows that records, or what came to be called statements, were envisaged only for those requiring special provision 'not normally available in ordinary schools', what has been called the '2 per cent'.

Warnock then goes on in the overview to suggest that the 1978 Report did not recognize the 'gradation of needs' nor the range of different needs adequately. Here she distinguishes between the needs arising from dyslexic difficulties, which she says could usually be met in ordinary schools, and the needs arising from autism and severe behaviour difficulties, which could not. More detailed examination of the 1978 Warnock Report shows that it did recognize the gradations and range of needs, but more of this in detail in the third section of my response. However, it is here that Mary Warnock attributes the 'tendency to overlook differences' to the concept of inclusion 'taking a foothold in society'. This is where she starts to criticize the 'ideology of inclusion' as implying the right of children with statements to be in ordinary schools. However, she does recognize that the legislation qualifies this right as subject to ordinary school placements not adversely affecting the learning of other pupils. But she claims that an adverse effect is hard to prove and reaffirms her assertion that 'disruptive children frequently hinder teaching and learning'. However, it is interesting that her argument shifts to talking about disruptive children, who are commonly taken to be a wider group of children, not all of whom would be considered to have special educational needs of a social, emotional or behavioural kind. What her line of argument also shows is that she is questioning the inclusive aspects of the special educational needs concept that connects children in special and ordinary schools and that integrates the needs of some with additional or different needs to the needs of all children.

This re-emergence of the importance of difference by contrast with commonality is then supported by reference to a tension or contradiction which she recognizes, following Alan Dyson (2001), between the aim of treating all learners as the same, while also aiming to treat them as different. This reference to the tension between a common and differentiated educational approach, which is sometimes referred to as reflecting dilemmas of difference, will also be discussed in more depth in my third section. It is however notable that she recognizes the tension and, rather than analyze various ways of resolving it, concludes that it generates confusion from which children are the casualties. Rather than consider how to 'include' children in a single institution while recognizing and responding to their differences as far as possible, she suggests that 'the desire to treat them as the same, and though a worthy ideal, it can be carried too far'. This is the key aspect of her position in this 2005 pamphlet; her criticism of what she sees as the 'refusal to address genuine differences' which she sees as having a negative impact on meeting individual needs.

Her easy giving up on, and lack of analysis of how to develop, the 'common' school, as one possible option, is evident in her examination of the option of setting up special schools or as she calls them 'specialist' schools. To justify this she outlines her criticism of what she calls the 'simplistic ideal' of all children 'under the same roof', a placement version of inclusion. She prefers a different concept of inclusion, where the ideal is about 'including all children in the common enterprise of learning, *wherever they can learn best*'(her italics). This is an interesting analysis because it highlights different aspects of the multi-dimensional concept of inclusion. However, in doing so, it opts for one aspect over the other without seeing how a placement definition ('under the same roof') and a curriculum definition ('common learning') can be combined. It is also evident that her concept of 'common learning' does not extend to the common social learning that comes from participating in a common learning institution. There is no recognition of the possible costs of separate institutions either in terms of experienced stigma for the children concerned and/or in terms of lost opportunities for their sense of social belonging to 'common' schools, as well as lost opportunities for other children to socialize and learn together as far as possible.

Mary Warnock then suggests a second type of specialist school in addition to current special schools for those children with significant and complex special educational needs. These are schools which will be smaller than ordinary schools, a school 'that is small and caters not for children with the most severe disabilities, but for those whose disabilities prevent them from learning in the environment of a large school'. The benefits of this smaller kind of school are described in terms of teachers knowing the children well, there being less bullying and engendering a sense of belonging. Though this idea of having smaller schools is a very important one, it is revealing of her assumptions that she sees them as being for children with disabilities and not for a mix of children with and without disabilities. She could have suggested that smaller schools be ordinary schools for the range of children's needs, but that they include children with less than significant and complex disabilities too. It is also notable that she says that such small specialist schools for children with less severe disabilities could be respected 'centres of learning' by specializing in specific subjects. This is an implicit recognition that special schools have been held as being having a lower status than ordinary mainstream schools However, this recognition does not lead her to 'hybrid' schools or any serious questioning of how the ordinary schools system can be reformed.

Historical background

Mary Warnock uses this section to explore the legal and conceptual history of special education since the Warnock Report 1978. She argues that her call for a 'radical revolution' in this field led by a government commission requires a historical account of the policy of treating all children 'as the same and treating them as different'. Her account of the work and recommendations of the Committee that she chaired is reflected in current perspectives on the Committee's thinking (Wedell, 2008). The main focus of thinking in the 1978 Report was to move away from 'what was wrong with the child' to what was needed for the child to make progress in learning. By including up to about 20 per cent of children in the concept of special educational needs, the 1978 Report was recognizing the links in the 1970s between those children in special schools (2 per cent) and those with difficulties and disabilities in ordinary schools (18 per cent). In this way the Report tried to 'normalize special education'. Here she recognizes what many involved in this field have recognized as the progressive and beneficial nature of the recommendations that were implemented through the Education Act 1981. This normalizing involved showing that there were children with different degrees of difficulties and disabilities, that some with more severe disabilities were already in ordinary schools, and that most children with difficulties and disabilities were already in ordinary schools. This focus on what was similar between all children in terms of shared educational goals was marked by the stress placed on the notion of a continuum of abilities and difficulties.

It is worth noting that this expansion of special education from the 2 per cent to the 20 per cent was also seen by some in the 1980s as the expansion of a system of negative labelling (Barton and Tomlinson, 1984). The Warnock framework was seen from this perspective as an ideological rationalization by policy-makers and professionals who had the power and vested interests in this expansion. The expansion was made possible by the linking of those with difficulties in ordinary schools to those in special schools (the continuum concept) which was used in ambiguous and tautological terms. This sociological critique highlighted that, despite the continuum of needs and difficulties, the Warnock framework still separated out the 20 per cent from the majority of children without difficulties in learning. The idea that the Warnock framework abandoned categories has been a superficial interpretation of the Warnock Committee's recommendation that: 'Statutory categorization of handicapped pupils should be abolished.' (Warnock Report 1978:

paragraph 3.25). This abolition was part of changing from more negative ('educationally sub-normal') to more positive sounding categories ('learning difficulties') as this excerpt shows:

> The term 'children with learning difficulties' should be used in future to describe both those children who are currently categorized as educationally sub-normal and those with educational difficulties who are often at present the concern of remedial services. (Warnock report, 1978: paragraph 3.26)

These recommendations led to the introduction of a super-ordinate category, a super-category, that of 'special educational needs' (Norwich, 1990). The point to note about this change is that it was not the abandonment of categories, but the switch between categories of child difficulties to a category focused on required additional provision.

I argued a while ago (Norwich, 1993) that the Warnock Committee's arguments for abandoning categories were weak and off the mark, a position that is still applicable. The Committee accepted some of the arguments of that period about categories – that some children had more than one kind of difficulty or disability, that categories stick and can stigmatize and that categories can operate as stereotypes promoting the idea that all children under the category have the same educational needs. Yet, the Committee did see the advantages of categories in focusing attention on the needs of vulnerable children, while also recognizing the disadvantage that categories could divert resources away from children in need who did not quite fit the category. What the Warnock Report did not do was recognize the tension between its recognition that categories offered a protection for the rights of children with difficulties to provision suited to their individual needs and its argument against categories:

> we believe that the most important argument against categorization is the most general one. Categorization perpetuates the sharp distinction between two groups of children – the handicapped and the non-handicapped – and it is this distinction which we are determined, as far as possible, to eliminate. (Warnock Report 1978: section 3.24)

This tension between protecting or assuring suitable provision for a vulnerable minority and the negative effects of labelling or categories gives rise to a basic dilemma about identification, reflecting dilemmas about difference that will be discussed in more detail in the next section. However, it is worth quoting an excerpt of the 1978 Report which indicates that the Committee was aware that it may not have resolved the question of labelling or categories.

> It will be argued that the practical effect of our proposal will be only to replace one label by another. We believe, however, that the term we have proposed, which will be used for descriptive purposes and not for any purpose of categorization, is preferable to the existing label because it gives more indication of the nature of the child's difficulties, and is less likely to stigmatise the child. (Warnock Report, 1978: section 3.26)

In context of this excerpt, we need to remember that critiques of the SEN concept were active in the 1980s (Barton and Tomlinson, 1984) and have continued to the present in terms of critiques of the 'medical model' as part of a particular kind of advocacy of inclusive education (Thomas and Loxley, 2001).

In her historical section Mary Warnock does then recognize some of the good aspects that came from implementing the 1981 legislation. This included it becoming easier, according to her, for parents to 'admit that children had many different special needs', that teachers became more interested in training to recognize and meet needs, that meeting needs in ordinary schools became better organized and school governors took on more responsibility for this. Yet, she also notes that this 'climate change' was not supported by extra government funding. In fact 1981 was a year when educational cuts had an impact. But, not only was the 1981 legislation badly timed, it contained what she calls the 'seeds of confusion' which originated in the 1978 Warnock Report. For her this confusion was over the desire to avoid 'categories of disability' which led to a 'tendency to refer to children with very different needs as if they were all the "same", i.e. special educational needs'. However, as I have discussed above, the Warnock Report introduced the SEN concept as a super-category while also referring to child difficulties in more positive terms, e.g. 'moderate learning difficulties' for 'educational sub-normal' and 'specific learning difficulties' for 'specific reading difficulties' (see Warnock Report, 1978: section 3.2.6). The main thrust of the SEN concept was to focus on identifying individual needs and this was represented in the statement that recorded special education provision for a particular child. The main change was, therefore, to how special provision was being represented. Special provision, since the 1981 legislation, was represented in terms of required goals, methods and placement, etc. for an individual child with special educational needs, and not categorized in terms of child disabilities and difficulties, as was the case with the prior 1959 Handicap categories (see Warnock Report, 1978: Appendix 2).

At this point in her historical section, she criticizes the language of need as if it was the opposite of the language of difficulties and disabilities. As I have argued, the Warnock report did recommend the continued use of categories, such as 'moderate learning difficulties', and examination of the terms of the 1981 SEN legislation indicates that special educational needs were defined in terms of children who had learning difficulties and disabilities (see the final section for more detail about this). She also criticizes the failure to 'distinguish various kinds of needs' as being 'disastrous' for many children. She gives as an example the different needs of a physically disabled child requiring a ramp for access and a child with Down's Syndrome who is prone to running away. These criticisms are hard to justify as there is little evidence that different needs have gone unrecognized. In the appendix to the 1978 Warnock Report, for example, the Committee recommends that statistical data about the range of special educational needs be collected in terms of the following nine broad areas: vision, hearing, mobility, physical health, language expression and comprehension, specific learning, intellectual functioning and social and emotional behaviour functioning. All these different areas were to be differentiated in terms of impairment, through slight, moderate, severe and to total impairment. A similar set of areas of special provision are set out in the first SEN Code of Practice (DfE, 1994). I suggest that the failure that she assumes did not exist, but that there was another failure; that provision required for these different kinds of needs was not always available in ordinary school or a mix of ordinary and separate settings. This failure is one that the House of Commons Select Committee points to in their recommendations (see the discussion in the previous section).

She then revisits her arguments from the previous section of the pamphlet about the 'disastrous legacy' of the 1978 Report, the concept of inclusion, a concept which has a 'remarkable foothold in society'. What is evident is that she does not ask at this point in her pamphlet why inclusion has established such a social position, nor does she discuss the fact that inclusion was a new term associated with political developments from the early 1990s after the demise of the Soviet Union and loss of faith in socialism. The way in which inclusion has been used in education and especially as regards children with disabilities and difficulties owes much to the political ideals of social inclusion, which were related to the values of solidarity, opportunity and becoming active participants in various aspects of social life. To attribute the hold of inclusion to the legacy of the Warnock Report over a decade before inclusion became a current political value is to ignore important social changes over the last three decades. Though there may have been some members of the Warnock Committee who supported closing all special schools in the 1970s, this was not the majority view then, nor is it now among many involved in the field (Cigman, 2007). Mary Warnock then claims that the 'official attitude' to special schools is 'patronizing' without saying whose attitudes are being talked about and who feels patronized. To assume that most children will be educated in ordinary and not special schools does not necessarily imply that special schools are 'little more than places of containment'.

It is interesting that, though she does not address the question of why inclusion has such an established position in her historical section, there are indications in her final inclusion section that she recognizes the significance of inclusion in wider social policy. In the third section, she explains that inclusion through its links to accessibility and widening participation is a basic concept and value across different areas of social policy.

She continues in her historical perspective by referring to the impact of the Education Reform Act 1988 on children with special educational needs; the pressure from school competition and league tables of attainment on schools' willingness and capabilities to provide for those who were more challenging to teach. The introduction of the first SEN Code of Practice (DfE, 1994) is presented as an attempt to redress the balance towards these children. This involved the development of school-based procedures for the identification of children with special educational needs without statements (the '18 per cent'), through stages which involved the participation of the SEN coordinator in developing individual educational plans (IEPs) with and without the support of external professionals. She also discusses briefly the introduction of the SEN and disability legislation in 2001 which introduced disability discrimination legislation to schools (not treating disabled children less favourably and making reasonable adjustments to prevent disadvantages) and increased the rights of children to attend ordinary schools.

Mary Warnock finally discusses in this section two aspects of the 1974 Committee which produced the Warnock Report that are of historical and current relevance. One was that the Committee was told by the then Department of Education not to include dyslexia as a special need. Her explanation of this is that dyslexia was then considered to be a 'fancy invention of the middle classes'. She writes that this did not matter to the Committee because their 'aim was to avoid labelling children as suffering from a named condition'. She then notes that dyslexia is a case of how 'labelling' creeps back as many children are openly labelled as dyslexic nowadays. However, though the Committee might have been given these instructions by government at the time and the Warnock Report might have not used the language of dyslexia, they did discuss this area of special educational needs in terms of 'specific reading retardation' (section 3.9), which was how children with specific difficulties in literacy were sometimes described. In their recommendations the Committee also referred to 'children with particular difficulties, such as specific reading difficulties, might be described as having "specific learning difficulties"'(section 3.2.6). I think the point here is that, despite Mary Warnock's use of dyslexia/specific learning difficulties as an example of the avoidance of labels/categories, less medically sounding categories were still used in the 1978 Report.

The second warning from the Department of Education that she discusses was that the Committee was not to count children who experienced social disadvantages or had English as a second language as having special educational needs. She attributed these prohibitions as stemming from the different responsibilities of different government departments; second language as a Home Office responsibility and social disadvantage as Social Services responsibility. She explains that this embargo meant that the Committee did not go as far as it would have liked to advocate special provision for children whose homes were 'impoverished'. She then claims that the 1981 legislation embedded this refusal to 'count social deprivation among the causes of special educational needs', something which she says looks 'absurd today'. However, there was nothing in the 1981 legislation's definition of special educational needs that could not include children whose 'learning difficulties' were mainly or partly caused by social disadvantages. This was unlike the case of children whose first language was not English, which was specifically excluded in this legislation as a cause of special educational needs (see Education Act 1981: section 2(4)).

It has long been recognized that many of the children with the difficulties which would now be called moderate learning difficulties and emotional and behaviour difficulties, would have experienced some form of social disadvantages. For example, the latest Department for Children, Schools and Families SEN statistics (DCSF, 2008) indicates that almost half of all pupils with SEN (48.9 per cent of the total with special educational needs at school action plus and with statements, some 665,500 pupils) had difficulties in the areas of moderate learning difficulties and behaviour, social and emotional difficulties. Though there are no statistics for these specific areas in relation to receiving 'free school meals' (taken as an indicator of social disadvantage), analyses do show that the proportion of pupils known to be eligible for free school meals is much higher for all pupils with SEN (school action plus and statements) than for those pupils with no SEN. For primary school pupils, free school meals are received by 12.6 per cent for those without SEN compared to 30 per cent and 24.9 per cent by pupils with SEN at school action plus and statements respectively. The corresponding free school meals figures for secondary pupils are 10.3 per cent compared to 28.2 per cent and 23.4 per cent (DCSF, 2008). This shows a disproportionate number of pupils having special educational needs come from socially disadvantaged backgrounds.

The SEN framework is compatible with an interactionist model of causation of special education needs, which assumes that environmental and child factors interact over time to result in the difficulties that give rise to special educational needs. (Wedell, 2008). So, we can expect that social factors will have an impact on the causation of special educational needs, and so interventions aimed at alleviating these disadvantages can be expected to impact on special educational needs, whether they are early pre-school intervention programmes like Sure Start or programmes aimed at specific groups such as children in care. Similarly, a high proportion of children in care have statements of special educational needs; of the 34,400 school-aged children in care in 2006, 28 per cent had SEN statements (DfES, 2006). But, a majority of those from disadvantaged backgrounds and children in care are not identified as having special educational needs. So, some of these children do not have sufficiently severe difficulties in school learning to be identified in the SEN system.

This analysis shows that identifying special educational needs is a school-based individual identification system. The planning that arises from it is at an individual level (the IEP and the statement) and so does not generate systems of provision which need to be developed through other means. That the SEN system does not relate to all children in care, for example, is because not all children in care experience the kind of difficulties in school learning that lead to special educational provision, in terms of what we currently call special provision. However, many children in care may need additional provision of some sort, as has been recognized and advised by recent policy initiatives (DfES, 2000). Schools are expected to have a designated teacher and to develop personal educational plans as a means of linking the support provided by social workers and others with that of teachers. This system is designed to provide additional support for the education of children in care, but it is separate from the SEN identification and planning system. The integration of different school identification and planning systems in terms of a generic 'additional needs' framework will be discussed further in the final section.

Statements of special educational needs

In the second section of the 2005 pamphlet Mary Warnock returns to the role of statements and examines in more detail the problems she identified earlier in her pamphlet: vague criteria for issuing statements leading to unequal provision and an overly bureaucratic system that causes 'bad blood' between parents, schools and Local Authorities. Some of the background to statements is then outlined including their expected function of protecting the interests of those who in the 1970s had just been given education rights, i.e. those with severe and profound intellectual disabilities. She then explains how the 1981 legislation did not specify which children in which situations would be issued statements. Because statements were issued in terms of the degree of special educational needs and not in terms of where children were placed, e.g. special schools, the Local Authorities had to decide on the threshold for statements and this introduced variability across the country. And, as more children with significant special educational needs were educated in ordinary schools, the question of who would be issued with a statement became more pressing. As Mary Warnock explains, parents who consented to their children's special educational needs being met in ordinary schools wanted assurances that the special provision would be available. Interestingly, although the first SEN Code of Practice (1994) focused on the procedures for statutory assessment and issuing statements, it did not address the question of which children would be issued with statements.

That there is statutory duty for Local Authorities to provide what is specified in the statement, but not to provide for those children without statements, has had the critical effect of bringing out tensions over special educational needs and provision between parents and Local Authorities. Parents would be inclined to see statements as a way of securing provision that schools and Authorities might not be making available. This is the socio-legal background to the growth of the quasi-legal system of tribunals to resolve disagreements between parents and Authorities. There are clearly hard choices faced by Local Authorities about how to spend their limited schools' budget; what proportion for the minority with significant special educational needs and what proportion for those with lesser special educational needs and all other children's needs. As Mary Warnock also points out, the reduced powers of Local Authorities did not help matters when schools began to manage their own budgets in the 1990s. Local Authorities had legal responsibilities for children with statements, but not always the power to implement their responsibilities. This increasingly became one of the main policy and practice issues in this field.

It is evident that Mary Warnock's critique of statements reflected a growing consensus that the system of statements was no longer fit for purpose, a position that was further endorsed by the House of Commons Committee Report and subsequent government actions. However, in this section of the pamphlet about statementing her arguments veer away from this focus and turn towards the question of inclusion, which was the main topic of her third and final section. Towards the end of the section she does return to the statementing question by referring to how the 2004 Government Strategy (DfES,

2004) dealt with statementing. As she points out, though the Strategy recognized the Audit Commission's identification of problems with statementing and the special educational needs system more generally, it failed to address whether statementing had outlived its usefulness. The government's policy pre-2005 was clearly to ignore the significance of these problems and its response to the 2006 Select Committee Report shows that this position continues. It is interesting that, though Mary Warnock is critical of statements, she does not consider the range of alternative options that might replace the current system. But, the one option that she discusses briefly at the end the second section is for statements to act as 'passports' to special schools. She indicates that this would be contrary to a policy of inclusion, implying that an inclusion policy is inconsistent with separate provision. The problem with this conclusion is that talking about statements as serving a different function, like access to separate special schools, would change the nature of statementing. It also does not examine the various elements of a statement and their current or possible future functions. I suggest that one of the reasons that the government has not confronted the system of statementing is the complexity of the different elements in the process and their functions. What is needed is an analysis of these elements, on one hand, and what the options are for retaining or abandoning them. How the system of recording special educational needs in Scotland (equivalent to statements in the rest of the UK) has changed illustrates one option. These will be discussed further in the third section of my response.

Inclusion as an ideal reconsidered

In this section Mary Warnock focuses on the concept and value of inclusion in more depth, after raising many issues about it in previous sections. Points about and against inclusion are scattered through her pamphlet. It is notable that while in some parts of the pamphlet she is very negative about inclusion[3], in others she is more positive about it ('the concept of inclusion springs from hearts in the right place', (page 32). This raises the question: does this reflect ambivalence about inclusion as a value? Taken with her recognition in the overview of the contradiction between aiming to treat all learners as the same and as different, is she responding to these tensions about commonality/ difference by dismissing them as 'confusion' (page 13) and closing down on a separatist resolution? I ask this question because her arguments for more special schools are that some children with special educational needs are bullied in ordinary schools and that these children are often physically included but emotionally excluded. Though there are clearly problems that need attention, there are other options for dealing with them. The first alternative option is to deal directly with bullying and social isolation at both an inter-personal level and systemically through whole school practices. Secondly, if there are structural issues about the size of schools that relate to the acceptance of and responsiveness to pupil differences, such as disability and learning difficulties, this is more relevant to secondary than primary schools. These problems might be ones that call for smaller and reorganized secondary schools. Here is a case of how the challenges that arise for special educational needs reflect on the quality of general provision and can be a useful source of school improvement strategies (Ainscow and Dyson, 2006). My point is that there are other options to pre-empting the establishment of more special schools. Some options may have general benefits for all children's social and academic learning, not just those with special educational needs. Nor does this examination of some of the options for dealing with these problems imply that there is no place for separate provision either in special units or schools.

Mary Warnock then returns to two of her key arguments about inclusion; that inclusion is about participating in the educational enterprise of learning and that school is not a microcosm of society. As regards the first argument, she asks the very relevant question of whether children with learning difficulties participate more in the enterprise of education when in ordinary schools than special schools? Her answer is that some children with learning difficulties and disabilities participate more in the 'enterprise of education' in ordinary schools, whereas others do not. This position is fine as far as it goes, but it does not go far enough into detail. It does not refer to the empirical evidence about social and academic learning outcomes in ordinary versus separate settings. Nor does it, despite her criticisms about not distinguishing between different kinds of needs, indicate for what areas of needs ordinary is better than separate settings and vice versa.

Reviews of empirical studies relevant to the outcomes of inclusive education over the last two decades have not been conclusive. In reviewing previous reviews from the USA and some from the UK, Lindsay (2007) concluded that by the end of the last century evidence in support of inclusive education was equivocal. Where it was positive in academic and social terms, it showed only marginal benefits and only for some areas of special needs. Lindsay's review from 2007 also concluded that there was still no clear endorsement for the positive effects of inclusion. However, and this is relevant to the kind of argument used by Mary Warnock in her 2005 pamphlet, neither was there clear evidence for the benefits of separate provision. Lindsay's conclusion is that more research needs to be focused on the processes and the conditions rather than locations that are relevant to educating various kinds of learning difficulties and disabilities. Another study relevant to the impact of inclusive education is the government-funded study of the relationship between levels of inclusion in ordinary schools (proportion of pupils with statements and at school action plus) on pupil attainment (GCSE point scores) (Dyson et al., 2004). The government was interested to find out if the presence of more children with special educational needs in ordinary secondary schools had any negative impact on attainment levels for all pupils. The analysis based on all English secondary schools found a very small negative relationship, such that higher levels of inclusion were related to slightly lower levels of attainment. Based also on school case analyses the authors concluded that this relationship was of marginal educational significance because of confounding factors in the analysis. But, they also pointed out that more inclusion was not associated with increased attainments for others, something that is sometimes argued in support of inclusive education.

Mary Warnock's second key point about inclusion as participating in a 'common educational project' relates to her assertion that 'school is not a microcosm of society'. She presents a particular view of education and school – education as a temporary phase, not a lifelong enterprise, and principles applying to society do not apply to school. Children are also represented as different from adults in needing help with their development. But these assumptions are stated rather than justified. The connections rather than the differences could be emphasized; school education as the start of a life-long education, schools embodying and promoting the principles of wider society and children and adults needing varying degrees of help with their development and well-being. But, her most interesting argument is that equality of opportunity might require taking steps in the present to ensure improved or equal opportunities later. As a principle this has been and can be used to justify specific interventions to produce desired future outcomes. But, to apply it to the justification for special schools or other separate provision depends on showing that the specific intervention, e.g. separate provision, does improve future outcomes. This part of her argument is missing.

Also, in arguing for inclusion as participation in a common educational project, and not 'under the same roof', she represents this educational project more in academic than social outcomes, and more focused on individual than social ends. This is implicit in her silence about why participation in the same local schools has been valued by many educationalists. The common educational enterprise can also be construed as including the social learning that comes from such direct participation and is not confined to learning in terms of a common academic-style curriculum. The statement of the common long-term goals of education set out in the 1978 Warnock Report can be used to make this point about a broader base for common learning, as this excerpt indicates:

> The goals are twofold, different from each other, but by no means
> incompatible. They are, first, to enlarge a child's knowledge,
> experience and imaginative understanding, and thus his awareness
> of moral values and capacity for enjoyment; and secondly, to enable
> him to enter the world after formal education is over as an active
> participant in society and a responsible contributor to it, capable
> of achieving as much independence as possible. (Warnock Report,
> 1978: section 1.4)

The first of the two general goals about intrinsic educational values goes beyond knowledge to include imaginative understanding and moral values. The second extrinsic goal refers to enabling active social participation and responsible social contributions. Being 'under the same roof', it could be argued, might be one of several conditions required for those with disabilities to learn to be active participants in society and for those without disabilities to learn to respect and appreciate the contribution of those with disabilities. So, it could be argued that both common educational goals call for schools to be places for the social experience of and interaction with different children and young people, including those with difficulties and disabilities. Participation in a common educational enterprise can therefore be connected to participation in the same school in terms of individual educational ends. But, a similar argument can be made by focusing on the social ends of education, which need to be linked to these individually focused ends. Schools are for reproducing moral, cultural and technical aspects of society, but they have also been seen as having some potential to lead and promote desired social developments (Lawton, 2004). Though schools are sometimes represented as not being able to compensate for society's problems, there is continued belief by many policy-makers and educationalists that schools can provide some useful leadership, for example in promoting positive images of and attitudes to people who are different from the majority.

Not only is Mary Warnock's attempt to differentiate between a common learning concept of inclusion and the common school concept of inclusion hard to justify, but her advice to ministers to consider the National Association of Head Teachers' definition of inclusion (NAHT, 2003), seems to ignore important aspects of the government's recent position. The NAHT conception of inclusion is as an entitlement of all to a broad, relevant and stimulating curriculum. The NAHT continues that all pupils are to be 'fully included in the life of their school community and which gives them a sense of belonging and achieving' (NAHT, 2003). She interprets this as supporting her position that inclusion is not where you are, but where you feel you belong. In fact, this position is not that different from the one that the government outlined in its 2004 Strategy (DfES, 2004) as the following excerpts indicate:

> Inclusion is about much more than the type of school that children attend; it is about the quality of their experience, how they are helped to learn achieve and participate fully in the life of the school. (page 25)

Later in the Strategy, the government recognizes that:

> Some special schools have felt threatened by the inclusion agenda and unsure about what role they should play in future. We believe that special schools have an important role to play within the overall spectrum of provision for children with SEN. (section 2.12)

As the House of Commons Committee concluded, the government has been inconsistent and lacking in specificity about its inclusion policy, but that is different from implying that the government has not recognized a continuing role for special schools in key strategy statements.

Mary Warnock then remakes a point made earlier in the pamphlet that one of the crucial changes that was needed was to break down the concept of special educational needs. However, the idea that special educational needs represented a homogenous group of children and young people has never been official policy nor the practice of Local Authorities, schools and teachers. Nor, as I have argued above, did the

Warnock Report fail to identify differences of need. It is interesting to note that even before the Warnock Committee was established, there was some legislation which required Local Authorities to provide for children with autistic and dyslexic difficulties (Chronically Sick and Disabled Persons Act 1970). As I have argued above, the problems in this field have not been about a failure to differentiate between educational needs, but one of not having a system for developing a range of appropriate provision that matches a clearly specified inclusive framework.

While recognizing that ordinary schools can be adapted to make them more accessible for some children, Warnock asserts that some children 'however much the environment is adapted' will not flourish in ordinary schools. There is little recognition in this kind of presentation of the historical continuum of provision in which there are various types of combination of in-class and withdrawal provision on site and off site of ordinary schools. Instead, there are general statements about children who are 'genuinely unable to learn in regular classrooms'. When she does refer to units, this is the 'concept of inclusion being stretched'. There is clearly a need, as part of a more specific inclusion framework, to clarify how units, separate or withdrawal classes operate. She then refers to school life in the playground or on the school bus being traumatic and introduces those with autistic spectrum difficulties as raising questions about inclusion. There has been an increasing awareness of the negative experiences of some of the growing number of such children and young people with these difficulties in ordinary schools. As Humphrey (2008) in a recent overview of the field has noted, research suggests that such pupils make easy targets for bullies, and are considered difficult to teach by teachers. Analyses have indicated that pupils with Autistic Spectrum Disorders (ASD) have been disproportionately excluded; they are more than 20 times more likely to be excluded than those without special educational needs.

However, where Warnock assumes that problems in ordinary schools make them inappropriate, Humphrey outlines evidence informed strategies to facilitate the 'presence, participation, acceptance and achievement of pupils with ASD in mainstream settings'. These strategies aim to challenge stereotypes about autism and raise expectations of their capabilities, help such pupils cope with bewildering noise and change in ordinary school activities, support peers to better understand how to relate to these pupils, change language use and adapt academic subjects. Another specialist in this field argues for an educational approach which draws on therapeutic ideas as well as entitlement ones (Jordan, 2008). Jordan argues that this requires greater flexibility and diversity in provision in which specialization has a key role in making inclusion work. This might mean that for individuals with severe autistic spectrum difficulties specialist support might be required, but not necessarily in separate settings. She refers to examples of provision involving resource bases: the child with ASD belongs to his peer group teacher but has the support of someone with expertise and there is a 'haven' when needed. Interestingly, Jordan sees a role for specialist schools for ASD less as havens to withdraw to and more as centres that actually pioneer new ways of working with ASD and dealing with the most extreme cases. As such these specialist schools would engage in research and training in collaboration with mainstream schools.

The above ideas about how to take account of the individual needs of children and young people with ASD are important for Warnock's general argument, as autism is one area of special educational needs where she interprets the problems in ordinary school provision as showing that more special schools are required. However, in this section of her pamphlet she also discusses how the specialist school initiative for secondary schools has been extended to some special schools which take on a specialist field, such as one of the four broad dimensions of special educational needs, e.g. cognition and learning, and as part of their role to support other ordinary schools in this area of SEN. She also refers to special schools taking on a specialism, e.g. in IT, and that these extra facilities are open to others who come to the school. However, in the case she cites they come after school and when they have left school and she reports no links between ordinary schools and this special school, such as are found in some formal partnerships between special and ordinary schools or in the co-location of special schools with ordinary schools. These hybrid arrangements seem to be the obvious way to connect the common educational enterprise concept of inclusion with the 'under the same roof' concept of inclusion that Mary Warnock wishes to keep apart.

In bringing this section of the pamphlet to a conclusion she revisits her position that one of the defects of the educational system is the size of schools. She suggests that the 'single most effective way to improve educational provision' for children who are 'fragile' and with 'learning disabilities' is small maintained schools. Statements would be required for entry to such schools and for no other purpose, so there would be no statements in ordinary schools as at present. However, she is vague about who would go to these new small special/specialist schools, if not those who already go to special schools, like the small special school she describes in some detail (designated for 'moderate learning difficulties' and with 156 pupils). There is some reference later on to children in care going to this new kind of special school, but it is uncertain whether she is envisaging all children in care going to such a school or only those 'in need' of such a school. This raises questions about how this would be defined and whether she considers there to be a need to extend the concept of special educational needs to include such categories rather than those having difficulties in learning and who may happen to be in care (see the discussion about this point above).

The alternative that she does not consider is the one that I raised before, that ordinary secondary schools might be reformed to become smaller, more the size of primary schools, and that parents could opt for this kind of smaller school. Preference might be given to parents of children and young people with learning difficulties and disabilities, but it would be open to all children. This flexibility in ordinary school provision might be, for some of the reasons she suggests to do with character and ethos, more appropriate not just for those who are 'vulnerable' or 'fragile', but suit the learning needs of other children too.

Concluding comments

In concluding this second section I want to draw attention to some of the key themes in Mary Warnock's 'new look' at special educational needs and inclusion. She reminds us that the original idea of special educational needs implied that some children are different or exceptional in being 'vulnerable'. From this she identifies:

> their right to learn that we must defend, not their right to learn in the same environment as everyone else. For them we must emphasize their differences, (i.e. their needs) as learners, not their similarities with all the rest.

I have argued that, though inclusion can be defined in terms of participating in the common enterprise of learning, it can also be defined in terms of participating in common institutions (i.e. local common schools). Though there may be tensions between learner-centredness and full-time participation in common classrooms for some children with learning difficulties and disabilities, it is possible to connect these concepts of inclusion through hybrid types of provisions. What is at stake is what is meant by 'learn in the same environment'. The 'same environment' might not be full time 'under the same roof', but clearly that depends on exactly what is meant by 'same' in this usage. Similarly, there is no simple polarity between focusing on differences or on similarities. It is possible to focus on similarities in some respects while focusing on differences in others. In the third and final section I will set out some of the options for resolving the tensions over similarity or commonality, on one hand, and difference/differentiation, on the other – what have been called dilemmas of difference.

3. What future for special educational needs, statements and inclusion?

In this final section I will examine questions which have arisen above, but will move beyond specific aspects in my comments in section 2 on Mary Warnock's 2005 pamphlet.

3.1 Has special educational needs outlived its usefulness?

In addressing this question I will examine various background questions about the concept of special educational needs.

The first question relates to some of the issues raised above, about what has been the assumed value of the term. It is worth restating that the term 'special educational needs' was introduced to move away from deficit categories – what the child or young person could not do – to what was required to provide learning opportunities and support learning. The assumption has been that the significant difficulties that give rise to special educational needs lie along a continuum. Difficulties are a matter of degree, with the difference being one of degree not of kind. The term is specifically an educational one that relates directly to teaching and learning. It contrasts with the related term 'special needs' which has tended to be used as a general cross-sector term. 'Special needs' like the term 'disability' applies across different areas of life activities, but 'special needs' has also been used to refer to needs beyond learning difficulties and disabilities, e.g. English as an additional language needs.

Another valued aspect of the special educational needs term that has been associated with the SEN framework in England has been the focus on individual needs. Identifying educational needs has in principle been by assessing individual functioning by reference to the person's particular context and circumstances. This has involved using an analysis of within-person causes (strengths and difficulties) interacting with contextual causes (supports and obstacles). This interactionist conceptualization recognized the combined role of individual and social factors and is consistent with the more elaborate and recent versions of a bio-psycho-social model of disability, as found in the International Classification of Functioning applied to children and young people (WHO, 2007). This kind of interactionist model is a useful way of going beyond the unnecessary polarization between medical (individual) and social models, sometimes promoted by some advocates of inclusion.

Though the special educational needs term was associated with these positive aspects, it did have some initial problems. As I have already argued above, introducing special educational needs was not an abandoning of categories, but a replacing of categories. Terms like 'educational sub-normality' were replaced by more positive terms like 'moderate learning difficulties', which has still been used as a category. The generic term 'special educational needs' came to operate as a super-ordinate category – or a super-category – covering needs arising from the range of more specific areas of learning difficulties and disabilities. The coverage of the term 'special educational needs' involved an expansion from the 2 per cent then in special schools to 20 per cent, the majority of whom had always been in ordinary schools. This expanded term might still attract negative connotations as did terms like 'handicap', as some commentators noted in the 1980s (Barton and Tomlinson, 1984). This expanded use of the term 'special' with its focus on individual needs also drew the criticism that all children could be said to be 'special' in the sense that everyone had unique individual needs. This criticism highlighted the ambiguity in the special educational needs term; was SEN about difference from the norm or about unique and individual needs (Norwich, 1993)?

When we consider how the term has been and is currently used since its legislative introduction, some of its weaknesses become evident. Though special educational needs was supposed to be about additional or different provision to meet individual needs, the term has come in its official usage to be synonymous with a child or young person's 'difficulty'. This can be seen in the way 'need' and 'difficulty' are used in the current SEN Code of Practice (DfES, 2001) and in the 2003 classification of SEN. Various categories or areas of general 'difficulties' are organized in terms of four broad dimensions called 'needs' (DfES, 2003). They are:

A. *Cognition and learning needs*
   Specific Learning Difficulty (SpLD); Moderate Learning Difficulty (MLD); Severe Learning Difficulty (SLD); Profound and Multiple Learning Difficulty (PMLD)
B. *Behaviour, emotional and social development needs*
   Behaviour, Emotional and Social Difficulty (BESD)
C. *Communication and interaction needs*
   Speech, Language and Communication Needs (SLCN); Autistic Spectrum Disorder (ASD)
D. *Sensory and/or physical needs*
   Visual Impairment (VI); Hearing Impairment (HI); Multi-Sensory Impairment (MSI); Physical Disability (PD)

Despite the principles of the SEN framework with its focus on needed provision (not difficulties) and on individual needs within an interactionist causal framework, we have here in official use a hierarchy of general pupil difficulty categories, with little reference to the child in context or individual needs or requirements.

With this background I will now outline some of the contemporary criticisms of special educational needs as a useful term. These criticisms may be related but for the purposes of this account will be organized under five headings:

1. Perpetuating negative labelling

This criticism is about SEN as a super-category with its continued focus on children's 'difficulties'. As a super-category the use of the SEN term continues to label children negatively and its use is devaluing of them.

2. As a poorly defined super-category

In this related criticism SEN is seen as poorly defined and vague. This can lead to uncertainty about the identification of special educational needs and results in a 'post-code lottery' about needs identification and therefore provision availability. Though Mary Warnock uses some of these points, this criticism is specific in pointing to problems in the coverage of the SEN term. If we compare the above English classification with the Organisation for Economic Co-operation and Development (OECD, 2000) definition of SEN below, we can see the weaknesses:

> beyond those who may be included in handicapped categories to cover those who are failing in school for a wide variety of reasons that are known to impede the child's optimal progress.(OECD, 2000: page 8)

'Special educational needs' for the OECD includes:

> *Category A*: educational needs where there is substantial normative agreement, e.g. blind or deaf ; organic disorders attributable to organic pathologies.
> *Category B*: difficulties in learning – not attributable to factors which would lead to categories A or C.
> *Category C:* educational needs arising from socio-economic, cultural and/or linguistic factors; some form of disadvantaged/atypical background that education seeks to compensate.

Comparing categories A, B and C with the DfES (2003) system (as above) shows that the four English dimensions of SEN relate to categories A and B; and that there is a silence about socially based needs seen to require compensatory education.

3. Separatist industry

This criticism focuses on the expansion of the SEN field by providers with a professional interest in a separatist field. This expansion can be seen as costly and inefficient, when what is seen to be required is improved teaching and learning in the general system.

4. Inconsistent with Common Assessment Framework

The Common Assessment Framework (CAF) has become a key part of Children's Services that are integrated and focused around the needs of children and young people in line with the Every Child Matters framework (DfES, 2006). The CAF is a standardized approach for practitioners in Children's Services (that have incorporated Local Education Authorities) to conduct an assessment of a child's additional needs and deciding how those needs should be met. The CAF distinguishes between children with:

1. No 'additional needs'
2. With 'additional needs'
3. With 'complex needs' who are part of the broader group of those with additional needs

Those in the second group, with 'additional needs', are said to include those showing disruptive or anti-social behaviour; overt parental conflict or lack of parental support/boundaries; involvement in or at risk of offending; poor attendance or exclusion from school; experiencing bullying; special educational needs; disabilities; disengagement from education, training or employment post-16; poor nutrition; ill-health; substance misuse; anxiety or depression; housing issues; pregnancy and parenthood. Children with 'complex needs' in the third group are those with 'additional needs' who meet the threshold for statutory involvement: children who are the subject of a child protection plan; looked after children/children in care; care leavers; children for whom adoption is the plan; children with severe and complex special educational needs; children with complex disabilities or complex health needs; children diagnosed with significant mental health problems; and young offenders involved with youth justice services (community and custodial). It is clear that the CAF incorporates the special educational needs as one amongst other statutory systems concerned with child protection, social care, mental health and youth offending. Though the CAF distinguishes between a wider group and one with more significant needs involving statutory procedures, how planning and services using the CAF will be integrated SEN and the other systems is unclear. This is an issue that the House of Commons Select Committee Second Report identified as requiring government clarification (House of Commons, 2007).

5. Fit with disability legislation

The extension of the disability discrimination provision through the 2001 SEN and Disability legislation also does not fit easily with the SEN framework. This is evident in the differing approaches to definition. In disability discrimination legislation a *disabled* person is defined as:

> someone who has a physical or mental *impairment which has an effect on his or her ability to carry out normal day-to-day activities*. The effect must be substantial (that is more than minor or trivial); and long term (that is, has lasted or is likely to last for at least a year or for the rest of the life of the person affected); and adverse (my italics).

In the SEN legislation a child has 'special educational needs':

> if he has a learning difficulty which calls for special educational provision to be made for him

A child has a 'learning difficulty' if:

> he has a significantly greater difficulty in learning than the majority of children of his age

or

> he has a *disability* which either prevents or hinders him from making use of educational facilities of a kind generally provided for children of his age in schools within the area of the Local Education Authority

And 'special educational provision' means:

educational provision which is additional to, or otherwise different from, the educational provision made generally for children of his age in schools maintained by the Local Education Authority (other than special schools) or grant-maintained schools in their area.

Disability in the one framework is about impairment having significant and adverse impact on every day activities. This is a cross-sector definition which relates to the second and rarely used part of the SEN framework in terms of a disability preventing the child using educational facilities. The primary definition and use of SEN is in terms of 'learning difficulties' that call for 'special education provision'; terms which were given open and relative definitions leading to some of the problems discussed above.

Having set out some of the criticisms of the term, some alternatives to 'special educational needs' will be considered briefly in these two options:

1. 'Additional support needs' or 'additional needs'

The Scottish system of 'special educational needs' and 'Records' of SEN has recently been replaced by a system of 'additional support needs' (Education (Additional Support for Learning) (Scotland) Act, 2004). 'Additional support needs' goes beyond the SEN concept found in the 2003 English classification of learning difficulties and disabilities to include:

any factor which causes a barrier to learning, whether that factor relates to social, emotional, cognitive, linguistic, disability, or family and care circumstances. For instance, additional support may be required for a child or young person who is being bullied; has behavioural difficulties; has learning difficulties; is a parent; has a sensory or mobility impairment; is at risk; or is bereaved... (Scottish Executive, 2004)

'Additional support needs' is more like the OECD (2000) definition of SEN and the CAF one of additional needs. In introducing a broader concept of 'additional support need', the Scottish system has also reduced the scope of the previous statutory system of Records, similar to statements in the rest of the UK. The threshold for Local Authority determined statutory planning – 'coordinated support plan' (CSP) – is to be confined to children and young people with enduring 'complex or multiple barriers to learning' who require a range of additional support from different services and not just in school. Coordination of the services is required where the Authority requires help from others both within the Authority itself, such as social work, or from outside agencies, such as health. The effect is that not all children and young people with additional support needs will have a CSP and many will have their needs addressed without one through school level individual educational planning.

'Additional needs' in the CAF resembles the Scottish concept in its distinction between the wider group of those with 'additional needs' and the smaller group subject to statutory procedures with 'complex needs'. However, though this system broadens the coverage for additional provision and promises to have integrated support and specialist services, it does not address some of the issues about the criteria for statutory assessment and issuing of 'statements' or 'plans', as the Scottish model does. However, it is too early to know whether the recent Scottish or the English CAF systems will result in similar issues to those experienced with the SEN term, as regards lack of specificity of coverage and the risk of it becoming difficulties and not provision focused.

2. Abandon individual model for the social model

This option rejects the above option which is seen to reflect an individual model in which provision is available for those whose educational functioning is significantly different from the norm. In a social model, disability or special educational needs is seen to be defined mainly by social barriers and prejudice. Though some people are recognized as having physical or psychological differences from a statistical mean and that these might be impairments, it is not these differences that are seen to lead to disability. It is society that fails to accommodate and include them in the way it would those who are 'normal'. So, in this option the focus is on ordinary schools making adaptations to accommodate all children and young people; categories of exceptional individual functioning will disappear as schools become more flexible and accepting of the diversity of learners.

However, the main and critical weakness of this option is that it provides no detail of how adaptations will be achieved. The denial of the impact of impairment – within-person factors – on learning is contrary to most concepts of disability, such as the one in disability discrimination in the UK and abroad. This option also avoids difficult and important questions about how decisions are made about when and for whom unusual and expensive accommodations are required, and on what basis the required additional resource allocations can be justified for some learners.

These two options can be seen to represent two stances to responding to learner differences:

A. A differentiation stance: that marks significant differences as 'difficulties' to focus on and ensure appropriate teaching adaptations.
B. A commonality stance: that responds to significant differences as requiring appropriate ordinary school and teaching adaptations.

Both stances can have risks; the differentiation stance can lead to separation, devaluation and stigma and the commonality one can lead to overlooking individual needs and inadequate provision. This sets up a tension that can give rise to a dilemma about identification that relates to what has been called dilemma of difference, a term used initially by Martha Minow (Minow, 1985; Minow, 1990). As Minow explains:

> When does treating people differently emphasize their differences and stigmatise or hinder them on that basis? And when does treating people the same become insensitive to their difference and likely to stigmatise or hinder them on that basis? (Minow, 1990: page 20)

In a recent international study of policy-makers', managers' and teachers' perspectives in the USA, UK and Netherlands about dilemmas of difference, I found that the majority of those interviewed recognized to some extent a dilemma about identifying children with special educational needs/disabilities (Norwich, 2008). Most of the participants across the three countries recognized tensions over identification between ensuring additional resources and avoiding devaluation and stigma. It is notable that their recognition of tensions was despite believing that there had been recent progress in promoting positive images of disability, that stigma had been reduced and that many parents wanted labels (Norwich, 2008: page 75). Participants in this study also suggested resolutions to the identification dilemma across the three countries which can be summarized as involving a combination of the commonality and differentiations stances being required, on one hand, with some residual tensions persisting despite these resolutions, on the other hand.

The general pattern of suggested resolutions was for commonality strategies, such as national and local developments that promoted an improved general school system that was more 'inclusive', with better training and improved school ethos. Connected to these commonality strategies would be ones that changed negative attitudes to SEN and disabilities through promoting positive images of disability and encouraging more social mixing and peer acceptance of children with disabilities. However, some residual identification of individuals was seen as necessary, but at a reduced level, some said for those with 'complex needs' using a 'minimal labelling' approach. When labels were recognized as necessary the suggested resolutions involved strategies that went beyond negative labels or terms, by focusing on individual and needed provision and showing sensitivity about labelling. Positive and open communications with parents and children were also seen as a way of reducing the negativity of labelling. Yet, some participants across the three countries recognized that identification tensions persisted despite these suggested resolutions.

Commonality and differentiation stances reflect particular value positions; commonality represents egalitarian and solidarity values while differentiation represents individual respect values. These values constitute a *plural values framework* which can justify a limited use of 'difficulty' categories. So, this framework will assume common or shared general requirements or needs for *all* children and young people. An example of such a commonality of needs in current policy would be the Every Child Matters five outcomes (healthy, safe, enjoying/ achieving, positive contribution and economic well-being)[4]. The values framework will also imply different requirements or needs relevant to the individuality of all children and young people, respecting each person's unique history and their balance of dispositions. I propose that designing specific categories or labels of difference be informed by this kind of values framework, and that there is less risk of negativity if difference categories are used in this values context.

Within this value framework it is possible to derive a conceptual model to inform decisions about categories. The identification of children who experience difficulties in learning that come under a particular title or label (such as having a disability, special educational needs or additional support needs) can be conceptualized as identifying additional general needs or requirements that are specific to a *sub-group* of learners. However, it can be argued that the particular needs of children in this sub-group go beyond the general needs of this sub-group. They also share needs or requirements with *all other children*, on one hand, and they have *unique individual* needs or requirements distinct from others in the sub-group, on the other. So, the identification of needs can be seen from this perspective to involve three dimensions (Norwich, 1996; Lewis and Norwich, 2004):

1. Needs common to all
2. Needs specific to sub-groups
3. Needs unique to individuals

Whether an 'additional need' category is required depends in this model on whether a particular child's needs can be identified and provided for by common systems that are also geared to unique individual needs. If it can, then meeting the child's needs will involve adequate levels of resourcing and teaching flexibility. But, if there are limits to resourcing and flexibility, then an 'additional' system for identifying and providing for a sub-group will be required. So, the need for categories of 'additional needs' and systems to provide for them can be reduced by improving common systems geared to individual needs, but limitations to the flexibility and resourcing of the common system will give rise to the need for such categories and systems. Categories and systems for 'additional needs' therefore depend on the nature of the common system and the learners' dispositions and capabilities.

Conclusions about usefulness of 'SEN' term

So, given the above position about some continuing but reduced role for a concept of significant 'functional difficulty', why would it be helpful to move away from the current concept of 'special educational needs'? The first reason is that a review and change would provide an opportunity to recapture some of the positive aspects of the original concept with its focus on needed provision and not just on difficulties. New terms could be introduced within a clear formulation of a values framework, like the one discussed above, and with a more explicit recognition of an interactive causal model. Using this causal model would imply being more specific about whether quality additional provision had already been tried and so discount contextual factors that might contribute to the difficulties in learning. A second reason would be that a new formulation of 'functional difficulty' in educational terms would enable a more explicit use of a 'response to teaching' model of assessment. This assesses learning and its difficulties in a teaching context and could draw on some of the UK and international developments in curriculum-based assessment of difficulties in learning. This assessment model is based on the general school provision being designed to be more responsive to all learner differences, not just those of children with 'learning difficulties'. However, there would still be some place for supplementary direct child assessment, often associated with health and some psychological assessments. A third reason for moving away from the current concept of SEN is that there could be greater clarity about the range of coverage of the terms, as we find in more recent developments, such as in CAF, OECD and Scots approaches, discussed above.

3.2 What future for statements?

As discussed above, there has been much criticism of the statementing system, but less analysis of the various elements in the system and what options there are for retaining or abandoning these elements. For this discussion the system of statutory assessment and issuing statements by Local Authorities involves three important elements:

1. Intensive multi-disciplinary assessment

This Local Authority system of assessment involves contributions from teachers, medical practitioners and psychologists. Other relevant professional contributions might also be included. Parents also contribute their own assessment of their child's needs.

2. Careful formulation of individual needs and required provision

The multi-disciplinary assessment then acts as advice to the Local Authority which through various means decides about issuing or not issuing a statement of needs and provision along with where provision will be available.

3. Legal assurances and procedural rights (annual reviews, tribunals)

Legal assurances to parents relate to procedural rights about various aspects of assessment, formulations of needs and provision, placements and reviews of statements.

Though much of the criticism of statementing is over unnecessary or inefficient bureaucracy, other criticism is about variations between Authorities in how they implement the SEN systems. These kinds of problems can be dealt with by improving the operation of the system and by clearer and more specification of procedures. They do not relate to the nature of the statementing system itself, which is about identifying the individual educational needs of children with significant or complex special educational needs. As an individually focused system, the end product of the system is a decision about provision for an individual. This is not a system for identifying the system of needed provision for a Local Authority and schools within it. So, what happens is that the system can generate a tension between provision seen to be needed (needed provision) and provision that is available (available provision). Without a system for also identifying and developing 'additional provision' at school and Local Authority levels, the kind of tensions and conflicts that have arisen between parents, teachers and Authorities, another major source of criticism of the system, are likely to continue. The House of Commons Committee's recommendations for minimum national standards for children with special educational needs, with some local flexibility, relates to this kind of analysis (House of Commons, 2006: section 255). The Committee also suggested a national statutory guidance framework that sets out expectations for schools and Authorities, so that there could be a broad range of flexible provision in the form of a 'provision map'.

So, any consideration of future options about statementing needs to see its dependence on wider changes in the SEN system overall. This is crucial when considering the following options, as some of them treat statementing separately from the wider provision system:

1. Current reduced statementing system

Government policy since its 2004 Strategy has been to reduce reliance on statements, leaving statements for those with more 'severe' and 'complex' special educational needs.

This has meant that some children with statements in ordinary schools, the majority with statements, have had their needs met through individual educational plans at school action plus. But, government has had to clarify with Authorities that it is illegal to have blanket policies about reducing statements. Pinney (2004) found that most children affected by reduced statementing in low statementing Authorities were those in the areas sometimes referred to as 'high incidence', that is specific learning difficulties, moderate learning difficulties, emotional and social difficulties. However, in these Authorities there were increasing proportions of children with autistic difficulties having statements, showing that reductions were not across the range. Authorities with this policy were found to engage with all parties in their strategic approach, delegate resources, support inclusion capacity building in schools and monitor progress of their strategy. However, whether a reduced statement system will avoid some of the tensions with parents over provision, as discussed above, is likely to depend on establishing an improved system of additional provision, as the Select Committee concluded (House of Commons: 2006).

2. Statements for special schools only

This was Mary Warnock's proposal in the 2005 pamphlet as discussed above. This might reduce statements by up to two-thirds, but whether it would provide assurances to parents with children in ordinary schools is another matter. It seems to be an option connected to an increase in special schools, as she recommends, not one that addresses the issues of appropriate and assured provision in ordinary schools.

3. Scottish model

The Scottish model represents another way of reducing the proportion of children's whose needs are met subject to specific statutory procedures and legal assurances. Rather than confine statements to those in special schools, as above, the 'coordinated support plan' with its statutory procedures will only apply to children receiving other non-school Local Authority professional or support services, for example children in care. This implies that children with severe or significant 'additional support needs' who do not also receive services outside the school will not have a 'coordinated support plan'. This model raises similar issues to those discussed about the above two options, about assurances for appropriate provision in ordinary schools.

4. Two-tiered system

In this option the first tier is the default system which has no statements or their equivalent statutory procedures and legal assurances while the second tier involves the statementing system, if parents decide that they want statutory procedures and legal assurances. In the first tier there would be individual educational planning with outside specialist support service assistance, as in the current school action plus system. This would apply to ordinary and special schools; transfers to separate provision would be negotiated directly between ordinary schools teachers, support services, parents and the receiving separate provision. If there are disagreements between parents and teachers and support professionals about needs and provision, then disagreement resolution procedures would be used and, if these were unsuccessful, then parents could invoke the statutory system and call for statutory assessment and other statutory procedures about formulating and reviewing statements. Appeals to tribunal would also operate as at present.

This option is on one hand more radical than the previous three options, but conserves the full statutory system on demand; it would extend the full range of specific statutory procedures and legal assurances to parents whether their children were in ordinary or separate settings.

5. Two-tiered system based on disability discrimination legislation only

In this option, the first tier would, like the fourth one above, involve individual educational planning as in the current school action plus system and apply to all settings. Disagreement resolution procedures could also be used but, instead of unresolved issues being dealt with through the statutory SEN system, it would come under the disability discrimination framework. There would therefore be no statements in this option, not even in a second tier. Statements would be abandoned and legal assurances could be in terms of schools' responsibilities not to treat a disabled child 'less favourably' *and*/or put the child at 'a substantial disadvantage by a school'. Many of the procedural problems with statutory assessment and statements would be dealt with in this option.

This option would replace the statutory responsibilities on Local Authorities for assessment and statementing by those placed on schools by disability discrimination legislation. This would focus responsibilities on schools which have not been subject to clear responsibilities under the SEN legislation.

Concluding comments about statements

It has been suggested that any system that improves on statementing, as it operates now, has to coordinate a national system of individual planning with a national framework for Local Authority and school level planning of additional provision. Without this coordination the persistent tensions between needed and available provision, which is reflected in the statementing system, will continue. Two of the options outlined above go beyond current practices and involve alternative ways to maintain legal assurances for parents. These and other options could be a way of addressing the continuing issues about statutory assessment and statementing. However, this could well reduce the incidence of disagreements but it cannot be assumed in proposing them that all disagreements and tensions over provision will disappear.

3.3 Beyond generalities for separate settings and inclusion

Mary Warnock's 2005 pamphlet has helped to clarify some of the differences in current perspectives about inclusion. One aspect about inclusion which can be overlooked in policy analysis is that for many inclusion is a 'passionate intuition' (Pirrie and Head, 2007). For some, their commitment to inclusion is deeply felt and self evident, while for others inclusion is about a political and social struggle (Allen, 2003). As a broad and significant social and political commitment it is often defined in terms of 'participation':

> the participation in the cultures, curricula and communities of *local* schools (Inclusion Index, Booth et al., 2000; my italics)

But, as indicated above, problems arise if issues over the definition of inclusion are not addressed. For a high stakes term which is supposed to make a difference to teaching and schooling, its definition and use are seriously problematic. The language of struggle, referred to above, implies that inclusion is a long-term project, which some present as a process. However, as a process it is not clear what the staging points are in this 'working towards' as the destination is left fairly open and vague. The effect of this framing of inclusion is that it becomes detached as a value from other values in school education. And, as such, inclusion can become 'a self-insulating process' (Pirrie and Head, 2007). Part of the problem is that inclusion is an abstract concept and value which is multi-faceted or multi-dimensional; there are various dimensions to it. This makes it hard to use the term and apply it in everyday policy and practice. These key definition problems were recognized by the House of Commons Committee when it urged the government to 'work harder to define exactly what it means by inclusion'(House of Commons, 2006: section 64). However, the government did not address this recommendation in its Response to the Committee (DfES, 2006), but merely stated that:

> The Government shares the Committee's view that inclusion is about the quality of a child's experience and providing access to the high quality education which enables them to progress with their learning and *participate fully in the activities of their school and community* (DfES, 2006: section 28. my italics)

What is notable about the government's and the Inclusion Index definitions of inclusion, is that they represent differing concepts of inclusion about placement (see italics in both excerpts). The government's focus is on an *inclusive system*, which could involve special schools, while the Inclusion Index focuses on *inclusive local schools*.

But the lack of clarity is evident even within the 'inclusive local schools' version of inclusion. What exactly does 'participation in local schools' mean? If children with disabilities spend *part of their time* outside ordinary classrooms, is that consistent with inclusion? And, if it is, how much separation is consistent with inclusion? Extending this line of questioning to being outside ordinary schools, are part-time placements in off-site settings for appropriate and time-limited learning compatible with inclusion? The point is that once some degree of 'withdrawal' from the general system is accepted, then this opens up questions of how far to go and when does this become exclusion? Set alongside these positions, Mary Warnock's position is quite clear; she rejects educational inclusion as 'all children under the same roof'. Withdrawal into special schools is acceptable because inclusion in this position is defined in terms of the commonality of learning: 'the common educational enterprise of learning, wherever they learn best.' (page 14)

All this calls for some analysis of why there are these policy uncertainties. I suggest that the same plural values assumption that was used to make sense of issues about identifying 'special educational needs' is relevant here. We are dealing with issues about:

1. Participation in local schools versus the general school system
2. Academic and/or social participation (social relationships and belonging)
3. Whether participation is compatible with the rights/requirements of the individual child versus the rights/requirements of other children
4. Placement versus curriculum participation.

Policy uncertainties about inclusion can be seen to reflect attempts to balance diverse values. To illustrate this we can focus on two general values relevant to educational provision, though these are not the only two relevant values:

Value 1 (individual respect): respond to individual requirements/needs of all children.
Value 2 (equality-community): promote a sense of belonging and acceptance in ordinary schools for all children.

The aim is to have it both ways; have arrangements that are consistent with individual respect and equality-community values. But, the question then arises for a plural framework about to what extent these values can be combined and coexist. Or does one value have primacy over the other? And, if so, which one? These questions cannot be answered in general as they relate to the specific kinds of 'differences' at issue (for example, whether it is specific learning difficulties or profound and multiple learning difficulties) and to the flexibility and responsiveness of schools to offer quality and differentiated provision. However, these values are linked to the commonality and differentiation stances discussed above and the balancing required to resolve dilemmas of difference. But, the dilemmas of difference we are dealing with here are not about identification, as above, but about what to learn and teach (curriculum dilemmas) and where to learn and teach (placement dilemmas).

In the international study of policy-makers', managers' and teachers' perspectives about dilemmas of difference, discussed above (Norwich, 2008), most of the participants across the three countries also recognized tensions to some degree over curriculum and placement issues. As with the identification dilemma, these were about common-differentiated curricula and common-differentiated settings or placements, where tensions in both areas could be about meeting individual requirements versus avoiding feelings of rejection/stigma and loss of equal opportunities.

Participants across the three countries in this study suggested some many shared resolutions to the curriculum and placement dilemmas which can be summarized as involving a combination of the commonality and differentiation stances, on the one hand, while still seeing some residual tensions persisting despite these resolutions, on the other hand. The most frequent overall pattern of suggested resolutions about curriculum tensions was for a balance of common and different curriculum aspects. This might involve modifying a general curriculum to meet diverse individuals needs, having the same general curriculum areas but designing differentiated programmes (more at secondary phase) and/or having the same curriculum objectives, but changing adapting teaching approaches. Some resolutions showed priority more to individual curriculum relevance, while others more priority to common aspects. Nevertheless, shared resolutions also focused on curriculum and teaching flexibility, with particular emphasis on special education and ordinary teachers collaborating, more time for some to learn and different curriculum focus for those with 'severe disabilities' on life skills rather than academic skills. Some participants saw continuing issues in these suggested resolutions, such as that some children and young people will have as much of a common curriculum as possible, but that some areas might have to be left out.

The most frequent overall pattern of suggested resolutions about placement tensions was for a balance of included and separate settings. The most frequent version of this resolution was to have a mix of settings which might involve flexible withdrawal. Other versions of this resolutions included part-time and short-term placements in different settings, use of resourced units or classes and better collaboration between ordinary and separate settings. Another frequent general resolution was about enhancing flexible services and staffing capabilities. Shared and frequently mentioned versions of this resolution included improved staff training, additional resources for ordinary schools, more collaborative teaching and improved planning of provision. As above, some participants saw continuing issues over placements, such as the gap between ideals and practice and differences among school staff in their commitment to the ideals.

Implications

The implication of the above analyses is that policy decisions involve striking some balance between commonality and differentiation stances in relation to various important dimensions of provision. Also, commonality and differentiation aspects of policies and practices cannot be detached from each other; the more commonality oriented policies still have some differentiation aspects and vice versa. This means furthermore that there are continuing risks of the negative consequences of differentiation and commonality stances. This means that there is no place for oversimplified splits or dichotomies too often found in debates over inclusion and should mean the avoidance of the futile pursuit of ideological purity.

What is needed, following this analysis, is a model of educational provision that:

1. Acknowledges tensions that can arise from sometimes conflicting values
2. Reflects resolutions where balance is sometimes required to have it all ways, as much as possible
3. Balances common and different/integrated and separate aspects
4. Recognizes the multi-dimensional aspects of provision, not just traditional focus on the continuum of placement

This is where Peter Gray and I have suggested a more elaborate model of provision relevant to the field of learning difficulties and disabilities, a model of *flexible interacting continua of provision* (Norwich and Gray, 2007). The dimensions or continua are represented in Table 1.

1	Identification	Whether and how children with special educational needs or disabilities are identified?
2	Participation	What kinds and levels of participation?
3	Curriculum	What do children/young people learn?
4	Placement	Where do children/young people learn?
5	Governance about educational provision	Which agencies decide about provision?

Table 1: Model of flexible interacting continua of provision

Some of the key options within each dimension can be examined by taking each of the five dimensions in turn:

1. Identification of children with disabilities and difficulties

The options below reflect different balances from the more commonality to the more differentiation oriented stances:

A. As part of an extended or adapted general system of monitoring and assessing learning progress and establishing individual or 'personalized' needs (e.g. using extended assessment systems like the P scales).

B. As part of a wider group of 'vulnerable' or 'at risk' children and young people with additional needs (e.g. as in the Common Assessment

Framework) as part of a three-dimensional model of needs assessment (common, specific and individual, as above).

C. As part of generic sub-groups of those with disabilities (functionally defined and informed by medical disorder categories where relevant to curriculum and teaching) as part of a three-dimensional model of needs assessment (common, specific and individual, as above).

The more commonality oriented the stance the more identification will involve options A and less B and C, while more differentiated oriented identification will involve C and B and less A. What is missing from this dimension is a fourth option, D, in which identification is in terms of medical/disorder categories. The reason is that such identification is too differentiated from the educational context of learning, though there is a place for such categories when they have specific educational implications and when parents and children's identity is related to medical categories, e.g. Autistic Spectrum Disorder, deafness and dyslexia.

2. Participation

This dimension involves participation in different kinds of activities and various levels of analysis:

A. Programmes and practices (kinds of activities)
   - Academic
   - Technical and vocational
   - Creative and social rituals
B. Social and cultural ethos (social-individual)
   - Organizational
   - Group/class
   - Inter-personal

3. Curriculum

The options below reflect different balances from the more differentiated to more commonality oriented stances to curriculum design:

A. Same general aims, different pathways/programmes, different levels in pathways and different (specialized) teaching approaches

B. Same general aims, same pathways/programmes, different levels in pathways and different teaching approaches

C. Same general aims, same pathways/programmes, similar levels in pathways and different teaching approaches

The more commonality oriented the stance the more curriculum programme design involves option C; the more differentiation oriented the stance the more it involves option A. What is missing from this dimension are options with consistent commonality or differentiation elements. The reason is that these options do not balance commonality and differentiation.

4. Placement patterns

The options below reflect different balances from the more commonality to the more differentiation oriented stances to patterns of placement:

A. Separate school (special school) and unit/class linked to ordinary school

B. Same school: part-time withdrawal to separate special school /unit

C. Same school and class (varying degrees of class withdrawal)

D. Same class (varying learning groups; no withdrawal)

The more commonality oriented the stance the more placement will involve options C and D and less A and B and vice versa for a more differentiation oriented stance. What is missing from this dimension is a special school/unit separate from ordinary schools option. The reason is that this option veers too far to a differentiation stance and not enough to a commonality one.

5. Governance and responsibility of separate settings (under national regulations)

The options below reflect different balances from the more central to the more local operational governance of 'additional provision':
Governance at:

A. Regional system of governance
B. Local Authority governance
C. Clusters or federations of schools governance
D. Individual schools

The more centrally oriented the governance, the more it will involve options A and B and less C and D, while more locally oriented will involve options C and D and less B and A.

What is distinctive about this model is that it contains several dimensions of provision that are interconnected. It does not just focus on placement as in the traditional continuum of provision (Norwich, 2008), nor does it consider inclusion as about curriculum and deny the placement aspects or focus on some aspects of participation, such as academic participation and ignore others, such as the social and cultural aspects. The interconnectedness of the dimensions is important for understanding the interaction between options across the different dimensions. Thirdly, the model sets some limits to the options within the various dimensions. For example, in the placement dimension the separate special school option is excluded as it does not represent enough of the commonality stance. Likewise, in the curriculum dimension there is no option with distinct aims disconnected from general aims for all for the same reason; insufficient regard to commonality stance.

A commitment to inclusive values using this model means that progress in developing educational provision is towards greater commonality in terms of all these five dimensions. The range of options included within each of the five dimensions is limited by a consensus about the balance of values and stances. In this version of the model there is no future role for separate provision that is disconnected from ordinary settings. Where there is scope for different positions and potential political disagreement is over the balance of priority given to the range of options. So, some might give greater priority to separate schools linked to ordinary schools than to same school part-time withdrawal arrangements. This kind of difference might reflect the political differences we could expect in current policy positions to school education. The point is that in a democracy these matters are political ones. My personal commitments are to exploring further prospects for a balance towards more commonality than differentiation, which differs from how I interpret Mary Warnock's political leanings. In supporting this balance to the common school that provides appropriately and sensitively for differences as far as possible, the challenge is to consider ways in which schooling, especially secondary schools, might become smaller and more responsive to differences generally not just for those with difficulties and disabilities. It is to development more hybrid provision, such as 'co-located' special schools and units that go beyond location to address wider aspects of participation.

My conclusion for this section is that going beyond generalities about inclusion and special schools is to see the future of additional educational provision as an interconnected one to a transformed general system. It is not one where additional provision becomes merged with and dissolved into the general system, a 'full' inclusion position, which I see as supported only by a minority. Nor is the future one in which additional provision is separate and distinct from the general system, which continues to be tempting to many others.

4. Concluding comments

Mary Warnock concludes her pamphlet with what she calls 'one firm conclusion' that there is a need for an independent government inquiry into the state of special education. We are awaiting (January/

February 2009) the outcomes of the Lamb Inquiry and the Ofsted examination of the field. Whether they will call for a more root and branch inquiry is one possibility, though these examinations may have been the government's way out to House of Commons Committee's calling for such an inquiry[5].

Nevertheless, I agree with Mary Warnock that a basic inquiry is required, though not from the same position. I have argued that there is a need for a clearer reconceptualizing of key aspects of the field in the light of changes since the 1970s and 1980s, in particular the concepts of special educational needs and inclusion, of the system of statementing and the need for a framework of educational provision that is relevant to plural values. I also agree with her that there is a need for more 'hard evidence' about the field. In my view there has not been enough intensive research into the policy and practice issues discussed in this response. Though there have been some government-funded studies since the 2004 Strategy, these have tended to be driven by immediate policy issues rather than longer term concerns to build knowledge and understanding. The conclusions of a review undertaken for the Audit Commission a few years ago highlighted these gaps (Dockrell, Lunt and Peacey, 2002), and there has been no major changes since then. There is much to be done.

Notes

2 and 5 The Lamb Inquiry was published on 16 December 2009, while this book was in preparation. The authors cannot therefore comment on it, nor on the response from the government. However, it is perhaps worth saying that this book deals with general issues, which are not addressed in the Report. For instance, the Report does not support a reviewing of the concept of special educational needs, as this is seen 'to divert energies away from more fundamental changes we seek to bring about in behaviour, attitudes and in the priority given to outcomes for disabled children and children with SEN.' Section 6.36.

3 Inclusion as a 'disastrous legacy of the 1978 Report' in section 1 and 'inclusiveness dictates that no art form should be encouraged, let alone subsidized, that is not popular' at the start of this section.

4 This ECM formulation of common to all outcomes, however, does not give prominence to social belonging and participation in its outcomes.

References

Ainscow, M. and Dyson, A. (2006), *Improving Schools, Developing Inclusion*. Abingdon: Routledge.

Allen, J. (2003), 'Inclusion for All? Beyond Support for Learning' in Bryce, T.G.K. and Humes, W. (eds), *Scottish Education*. (2nd edition) Edinburgh: University of Edinburgh.

Audit Commission (1992), *Getting into the Act*. London: HMSO.

Audit Commission (2002), *Statutory Assessment and Statements: In Need of Review?* London: Audit Commission.

Barton, L. and Tomlinson, S. (1984), 'The Politics of Integration' in Barton, L. and Tomslinson, S. (eds), *Special Education and Social Interest*. Buckingham: Croom Helm.

Booth, T., Ainscow, M. and Black-Hawkins, K. (2000), *Index for Inclusion: Developing Learning and Participation in Schools*. Bristol: CSIE.

Cigman, R. (2007) (ed.), *Included or Excluded? The Challenge of the Mainstream for Some Children with SEN*. London: Routledge.

DCSF (2008), *Statistical Release: SEN Statistics*. SR 15/2008 DCSF.

DCSF (2009), *Lamb Inquiry: Special Educational Needs and Parental Confidence*. London: DCSF, available at www.dcsf.gov.uk.

DfE (1994), *Code of Practice: Identification and Assessment of Special Educational Needs*. London: DfE.

DfES (2000), *Guidance on the Education of Children and Young People in Public Care*. London: HMSO.

DfES (2001) *Code of Practice for the Identification and Assessment of Special Educational Needs*. (Revised) London: DfES.

DfES (2003), *Data Collection by Type of Special Educational Needs*. London: DfES.

DfES (2006), *Outcome Indicators for Looked after Children. Twelve Months to 30 September 2006*. London: DfES.

DfES (2004), *Removing Barriers to Achievement: SEN Strategy*. London: DfES.

DfES (2006), *Government Response to Education and Skills Committee Report on Special Educational Needs* (Cm 6940). London: DfES.

DfES (2006), *The Common Assessment Framework for Children and Young People: Practitioners' Guide*. Annesley, DfES.

Dockrell, J., Lunt, I. and Peacey, N. (2002), *Literature Review: Meeting the Needs of Children with Special Educational Needs*. London: Audit Commission.

Dyson, A. (2001), 'Special Needs in the Twenty-first Century: Where We've Been and Where We are Going', *British Journal of Special Education* 28, 1, 24–29.

Dyson, A., Farrell, P., Polat, F., Hutcheson, G., and Gallannaugh, F. (2004), *Inclusion and Pupil Achievement* (Research Report RR578). Nottingham: Department for Education and Skills.

House of Commons Education and Skills Committee (2006), *Special Educational Needs. Third Report of Session 2005–06*. London: Stationery Office.

House of Commons Education and Skills Committee (2007), *Special Educational Needs: Assessment and Funding*. London: Stationery Office.

Humphrey, N. (2008), 'Including Pupils with Autistic Spectrum Disorders in Mainstream Schools'. *Support for Learning*, 23, 41–48.

Jordan, R. (2008), 'Autistic Spectrum Disorders: a Challenge and a Model for Inclusion in Education'. *British Journal of Special Education*, 35, 1, 11–15.

Lawton, D. (2004), *Education and Labour Party Ideologies, 1900–2001 and Beyond*. London: RoutledgeFalmer.

Lewis, A. and Norwich, B. (2005), *Special Pedagogy for Special Children? Pedagogies for Inclusion* (eds), Maidenhead: Open University Press.

Lindsay, G. (2007), 'Educational Psychology and the Effectiveness of Inclusive Education/Mainstreaming'. *British Journal of Educational Psychology*, 77, 1–24.

Minow, M. (1985), 'Learning to Live with the Dilemma of difference: Bilingual and Special Education' in Bartlett, K.T. and Wegner, J.W. (eds) *Children with Special Needs*. Boulder: Transaction Books.

Minow, M. (1990), *Making All the Difference: Inclusion, Exclusion and American Law*. Ithaca: Cornell University Press.

NAHT (2003), *Policy Paper on Special Schools*. www.naht.org.uk.

Norwich, B. (1990), *Reappraising Special Needs Education*. London: Cassell.

Norwich, B. (1993), 'Has "Special Educational Needs" Outlived its Usefulness?' in Visser, J. and Upton, G. (1993), *Special Education in Britain after Warnock*. London: David Fulton Publishers.

Norwich, B. (1996), 'Special Needs Education, Inclusive Education or Just Education for All?' (Inaugural Lecture). Institute of Education, University of London.

Norwich, B. and Gray, P. (2007), 'Special Schools in the New Era: Conceptual and Strategic Perspectives' in *Special Schools in a New Era: How Do we Go Beyond Generalities?* Special Educational Needs Policy Options Paper 2, series 6, www.nasen.org.uk.

Norwich, B. (2008), *Dilemmas of Difference, Inclusion and Disability: International Perspectives and Future Directions*. London: Routledge.

OECD (2000), *Special Needs Education: Statistics and Indicators*. Paris: OECD.

Ofsted (2004), *Special Educational Needs and Disability: Towards Inclusive Schools*. London: Audit Commission.

Ofsted (2006), *Inclusion: Does it Matter Where Pupils are Taught? Provision and Outcomes in Different Settings for Pupils with Learning Difficulties and Disabilities*. HMI 2535.

Pinney, A. (2004), *Reducing Reliance on Statements: an Investigation into Local Authority Practice and Outcomes*. Research Report 508. Nottingham: DfES.

Pirrie, A. and Head, G. (2007), 'Martians in the Playground: Researching Special Educational Needs'. *Oxford Review of Education*, 33, 1, 19–31.

Scottish Executive (2004), *Summary Handout on the Additional Support for Learning Act*. Education Department.

Thomas, G. and Loxley, A. (2001), *Deconstructing Special Education and Constructing Inclusion*. Buckingham: Open University Press.

Visser, J. and Upton, G. (1993), *Special Education in Britain after Warnock*. London: David Fulton Publishers.

Wedell, K. (2008), 'Evolving Dilemmas about Categorization' in Florian, L. and McClaughlin, M. (eds) *Disability Classification in Education: Issues and Perspectives*. Thousand Oaks: Corwin Press.

WHO (2007), *International Classification of Functioning, Disability and Health*. Geneva: World Health Organisation.

Response to Brahm Norwich

3

Mary Warnock

As Brahm Norwich says at the beginning of his response, much has happened in the field of special educational needs since the publication of my pamphlet. Indeed it is difficult to keep the chronology of change clear in one's head, so numerous have been the initiatives, reports and government responses to reports since then. The first part of Norwich's response sets out, with lucidity and fairness, what has happened since 2005. I would add only a few words about what provoked the pamphlet in the first place.

The pamphlet was written early in 2005 in response to a request from Ruth Cigman, one of the editors of the Impact series for the Philosophy of Education Society at London University. She and I knew each other of old, and we had met again in 2004, and discussed SEN. We worked together very closely on the pamphlet, she often attempting to tone down my somewhat intemperate language. For the pamphlet was intended to be a polemic. I had become increasingly aware of the inequalities of provision for children and young people with special educational needs, of the time-wasting bureaucracy often involved, especially in the issuing of statements, of the essential ambiguity in the attitudes of successive ministers towards special schools, and of the frustration and near desperation of many parents, frequently leading to a sadly confrontational attitude towards Local Authorities, made worse by the widely varying practices of the Authorities themselves. I was conscious, too, of the new dimension of ambiguity caused by the Special Educational Needs and Disability Act 2001, which sought to carry over from the earlier Disability Discrimination Act a statutory right for children with disabilities not to be treated worse than their contemporaries at school on account of their disability alone. The very definition of 'disability' was lifted from the earlier act which had been concerned with discrimination in the workplace and with the equal provision of public services, and had had nothing specifically to do with education. The relation between a disability and an educational need was becoming increasingly obscure. Moreover it seemed that under the 2001 Act, a criminal charge hung over a school, or its head, if they refused entry to a child on account of his 'disability' or if, having admitted him, they subsequently excluded him. The mismatch between disability and educational need had become especially obvious in the case of those children assessed as having emotional and behavioural difficulties, those who used to be referred to as the maladjusted. This condition, only dubiously to be called a disability at all, was related specifically to childhood and to school, needed a specifically educational response, often in a specialized environment, which would gradually enable the child to learn, and perhaps return to ordinary school. It was distorting the concept of children's rights to suppose that a child's rights had been infringed if he were excluded from a mainstream school where his disruptive behaviour was hindering the learning of other children as well as his own. I shall return to this crucial issue at the end of my response (page 138).

As a polemic, the pamphlet probably worked quite well, though a great deal of unproductive pseudo-excitement was generated by those newspapers devoted to the search for scandal, who detected a u-turn, one of their favourite events, in my personal position with regard to the inclusion of children with special needs in mainstream schools. I was especially savagely attacked by the journalist Melanie Phillips, for first having ruined the educational chances of children with disabilities by insisting they be integrated in mainstream schools and for then blithely changing my mind after the damage had been done. I am grateful to Brahm Norwich for denying such a turn and he rightly points to my misgivings about the more hard-line inclusionists as long ago as 1993.

It is perhaps worth pointing out that people are prone to attribute the recommendations of Committees of Inquiry to the sole authorship of their chairman, and presume that every nuance of their reports reflects the chairman's personal convictions. Of course this is misleading. A good Committee of Inquiry comes up with a consensual report, and individual members of the committee, including its chairman, may have reservations or qualifications not necessarily shared by all members. However I do not deny that the chairman of a Committee of Inquiry whose name is attached to the report has to take final responsibility for its contents.

In this instance I know that I and the member of the committee who was a psychiatrist, specializing in adolescence, believed that children with emotional and behavioural problems would be very hard to accommodate in the mainstream and many would need special schools, some with boarding facilities, if they were to be brought to a position where they could begin to learn, without preventing others learning. (We also both had reservations about whether parents could always be treated as partners, as a chapter in our report suggested. In the case of some children with special needs their difficulties were largely attributable to their parents from whose influence schools must somehow try to release them.) Nor did our report recommend that the most severely mentally and multiply disabled children should not attend special schools. We even recommended what is now government policy, namely that special schools should become resource centres and centres of learning and training for teachers, including teachers in the mainstream.

Thus in 1978 we certainly did not recommend that special schools should be phased out, though this was at the time the wish of some individual committee members and, of course, remains the goal of some of the disability lobby, such as the 20/20 group, today. So there was no u-turn, and this particular issue is a distraction from the ongoing history of SEN provision. This is clearly acknowledged by Brahm Norwich at the beginning of his Introduction (page 49) and need not be further discussed.

In any case, on 22 June 2005 Barry Sheerman, the Chairman of the House of Commons All Party Select Committee on Education declared in the House of Commons that, partly in consequence of my pamphlet, he would put the topic of SEN at the top of his list of topics to be discussed by his committee, should he be re-elected as chairman, (Hansard 22 June: col. 844), and the following week David Cameron, then Shadow Education Minister, spoke at the launch of the pamphlet in the Senate House of the University of London. In the event, David Cameron was elected leader of his party soon afterwards and no longer publicly spoke much about education, though retaining his deep interest in it. Barry Sheerman was re-elected chairman of the All Party Select Committee and kept his word, their report on SEN appearing in June 2006. The report echoed the main recommendation of my pamphlet, that there should be a thoroughgoing new examination of provision for special educational needs, a recommendation that the government rejected. The Select Committee also concluded that the concept of the statement was no longer fit for purpose, and also that any formal assessment of children's needs should be carried out by an independent body, separate from the Local Authority who had to fund the necessary provision. This too was rejected by government, though it is an obviously desirable reform. The dual role of Local Authorities in assessing for statements and paying for extra provision plainly renders the statement at best a partial reflection of a child's educational needs, depending as it does on what the Local Authority thinks it can afford.

There is one point raised by Brahm Norwich for which I can only apologise not only to him, but to any other readers of the pamphlet. Near the beginning, (page 12), in the Overview, I said that the number of children with statements was nearly 20 per cent of school-age children. We did, as a committee, underestimate the number of statements that would be issued, but the average figure never rose even as high as 4 per cent. However, the point I failed to make, as a result of careless proofreading, was that average percentage figures were not of much use in estimating the number of statements issued, because, while some Local Authorities, such as Stockport, hardly gave any children statements, others, mostly in the South, were more lavish.

History does not come to an end and, at the time of writing, a new government-commissioned report is expected from Brian Lamb, to be published in the autumn of 2009[6]. And there is to be another Ofsted report as well. It is extremely difficult to predict what changes may be on the way. But it seems clear that the present government, at least, is committed to piecemeal, rather than radical, reform of the education of those with special needs, and I remain of the opinion that this is a mistake.

I still very much hope that in the foreseeable future there will be a new Committee of Inquiry. This might lead to the setting up of an (unfashionable) standing Royal Commission, charged with the task of carrying out a series of investigations of aspects of education, on the model of the Royal Commission on Environmental Pollution. Such a Commission would work very much in the way that the House of Commons All Party Select Committee works, but would be apolitical, not troubled by any question of party loyalties.

Thinking about the kinds of issues that such a Commission might address, there is one matter (among many others) on which I am completely in agreement with Brahm Norwich, and that is that questions about the education of children with special needs cannot any longer be treated as a separate issue, detached from questions about education as a whole. This is especially true if one is considering secondary school education. It has nothing specifically to do with the education of those with SEN. Rather, one of the things that has most strikingly changed since 1978, and indeed even since 2005, is the extent to which secondary schools are agreed to be failing to educate a large proportion of their pupils, whether they are assessed as having special educational needs or not. The reason why my committee did not address this problem was partly that things were perhaps not so bad then as they are now (or were not so obviously bad) but also because we were instructed by the then Department of Education that we were not to consider as 'handicapped' those who were suffering from social deprivation. This embargo was reflected in the 1981 Act, which expressly excluded from consideration as having special needs those children, for example, for whom English was not their first or their home language. Such division between different kinds of educational needs may indicate how civil servants secretly clung to the old medical model of 'handicap'; in any case today it seems ludicrous. For social reasons largely beyond their control there are many schools, both primary and secondary, where the education of the majority of pupils is compensatory or remedial, attempting to make up for deprivation at home. Such deprivation is often experienced by children who are not living in poverty, but are deprived of proper conversation with adults, and who spend too much time isolated with their television sets or computer games. Their educational needs are great, but perhaps not 'special'.

My 2005 pamphlet was very low on suggestions for what might be done to resolve the 'dilemma of difference', as it has come to be called. (And Brahm Norwich expounds this dilemma with particular force, see page 91.) Are children with special educational needs to be educated as if they were the same as their fellow pupils, or as if they were different, and different, too, from one another, each with individual needs that must be met, if they are to flourish? The reason for this reticence on my part was that I genuinely believed then, as I do now, that what we need is not a few bright ideas, but a serious evidence-based analysis of what is wrong with the present system, and how resources can be better used to improve secondary school education in general, not only for those with special needs. Far too many young people leave school, many of them simply giving up attending before the school-leaving age, completely at odds with everything that school offered them. Young people are now committing a criminal offence if they are not in any form of education or apprenticeship between the ages of 18 and 24. The parents of those aged between 14 and 16 have long been liable to a charge if their children are not attending school, and the school-leaving age has now been raised to 18. These young people are perhaps the most worrying and hopeless group of all, whether or not their needs are deemed 'special'. Whatever their assessment was when they still regularly attended school, there is no doubt that at this age they most certainly have the need to be educated in a way that is acceptable to them, and that will be useful for their future.

The government, in my view disastrously, rejected the recommendations of Mike Tomlinson for the reform of education for students aged from 14–19. They seem astonishingly timid when faced with the possibility of radical change. In this case the change proposed was the abandonment of A levels, and the introduction instead of an overarching school leaving certificate, including records of both practical and academic achievement, but with the possibility of pursuing a wholly practical or vocational course from the age of 14, as well as a wholly academic or a mixed course. Pupils could take modules of these qualifications at any age at which they were ready. They could thus take responsibility for their own progress, and not automatically work always with their own age group. The government however insisted that A levels remain, but that new qualifications should be introduced alongside A levels, (the gold standard, as they increasingly implausibly averred, a phrase unhappily taken over from the Tory Education Minister, Kenneth Baker). These qualifications should indeed be less academic than A levels, but should have 'parity of esteem'. It seems that they had learned nothing from history in making such a proposal. For there is a yearning for the academic that seems to be wired into those who make educational policy, as well as into many parents and, of course, more properly, into universities. It was this yearning, a kind of vestigial snobbishness, a Platonic scorn for manual workers, that made the attempt in the 1940s to introduce three kinds of school, the grammar, the technical and the secondary modern, such a conspicuous failure. These three sorts of schools were also supposed to command parity of esteem. But of course they did not, and the technical schools soon dropped out of existence, leaving the secondary modern deemed of 'bog standard' and in urgent need of rescue. As long as academic qualifications exist separately, they will be judged better than any other qualifications, and this despite the fact that plumbers can earn far more than professors. In this country there remains the phenomenon that used to be known as 'academic drift'. This expression was used in the 1980s to denote the tendency in the then polytechnics to spend more and more of their resources on non-technical education and, even where subjects were technical or practical, they were so taught as to introduce an academic or theoretical element in all their courses. This came about because some polytechnics had begun to award degrees at the end of their courses, and there was a body which oversaw the degree-awarding process, indeed which actually awarded the degrees itself. This was the CNAA, the Council of National Academic Awards. I was a member of this body for many years and our task was to ensure that all courses that led to CNAA degrees were of 'degree standard'. I need not go on about the inherent absurdity of this system. But academic drift was confirmed and legitimized when the polytechnics became universities in 1993.

The new qualifications are an attempt to reverse our habitual intellectual snobbishness, but they will almost certainly fail as long as they remain separate from each other. In any case the recession is not helpful to the enterprise of deeming work experience or apprenticeships to be part of education. Few employers can afford the expensive luxury of apprenticeships. However, I believe that we cannot go on as we are. Secondary education in the maintained sector has never seemed more obviously to lag behind that in independent schools. Any change that engaged the interest of secondary school students who are not interested in or capable of engaging in the abstract or the theoretical, who need hands-on, bottom–up learning would be of immense advantage to those who are at present designated as having learning difficulties, or indeed behavioural problems.

Tomlinson also recommended as part of his reforms that there should be a new style of teaching and learning for the 14–19 age group. He argued that pupils could be grouped together according to how far they had progressed in a particular subject rather than always working with their age group. So a particularly skilled and successful mechanic could rise up the ladder of qualifications, overtaking others of his age, rather in the way that music students can take the different grades of the Associated Board or Trinity College examinations when they are ready. This would be of great advantage to both the academic and the practical pupils, and would mean that they would learn as much from one another as from their teachers. It would also greatly help those regarded as having learning difficulties. The struggle to keep up with the pace of the class as a whole would be diminished, and the strategy would fit with the government's declared intention to introduce 'personalized' learning.

Tomlinson's recommendations were premised on good teaching of basic skills at primary school. This itself requires that the natural desire to learn that most primary school children have, whatever their abilities, should not be stifled or deflected by rigid teaching in preparation for tests. And there should be far more expertise among primary school teachers to enable them to identify children with specific learning difficulties from reception age and Year 1 onwards, so that these children may be given professional support, not merely support from untrained classroom assistants. Both the Audit Commission and Ofsted found that too often this was the fate of children who desperately needed the benefit of experienced and, above all, specialized teachers. Early expert intervention is absolutely essential if dyslexic children, for example, are to be able to function successfully as they move up the school. The government has been persuaded of this, and has undertaken that there must be changes in initial teacher training that will equip ordinary teachers better to know when to call in help, and also that every primary school child must have access to a specialist teacher, when required. If these undertakings are honoured, it should mean a substantial reduction in future years of children deemed to have special educational needs, which were after all originally defined as needs that a school could not meet within its ordinary resources. But it is not clear whether or not in the current economic climate such measures will be continued.

There are ways, then, in which the number of children assessed as having special educational needs could be diminished, whether by a radical change in the system of school-leaving qualifications, or by early specialist intervention, or by both. This leads to the central and most fundamental question raised by Brahm Norwich's response: the question of 'special educational needs' as a framework concept, a Kantian Category of the Understanding, if I may put it like that. There is no doubt that in the minds of ministers, civil servants and probably most of the teaching profession, SEN has indeed become an element in the way they organize and give shape to the educational world, as essential to thought as Kant's categories of, say, causation or substance, as essential to educational thought as the concepts of teaching and learning themselves. But do we any longer need the concept? Could we, as the Scots have, abandon the words? (I would like to have evidence from Scotland, which I am sure is accumulating as time passes, but of which I am ignorant.) The issue is precisely that of the Dilemma of Difference, first identified by Martha Minow (1990), and developed in education by Brahm Norwich (1996) and Alan Dyson (2001) and, as I have said, forming an integral place in Norwich's response (page 91).

I now see that the 1978 report, which as Norwich says, recognized the dilemma of difference, dealt with it only at a very superficial level. In our defence, I suppose I would plead that at the time the committee faced two urgent problems. The first was how to bring into education those profoundly disabled children who had hitherto been outside the system altogether; the second was to call attention to the continuum of ability/disability already in mainstream schools. There had to be devised some way of referring to the conjoined class of all these children, different as they were individually one from another, because we were asking the government to legislate to ensure that public funds were spent on all of them. We had to find a way to designate them, but of course in so doing we set them apart. We were trying, as Norwich clearly sees, simultaneously to make them the same as and different from the rest. Obviously this was an impossible task.

I think that this aim, though in some sense contradictory, was what was intended to constitute the force of our word 'integration'. When we spoke of the integration of children with special needs into mainstream schools we had in mind the possibility of children who were different from one another living peacefully beside those from whom they were different, their differences recognized, that is to say, but not so much insisted on as to set them totally apart. This would, we hoped, mean that different teaching strategies, different teaching styles, could coexist in the same schools, and even in the same classrooms. I shall return to the concept of integration and that of inclusion below.

The superficiality of our approach is reflected in our belief (it seemed exciting and missionary at the time) that we could 'abolish categories' or avoid 'labelling'. I have to say that I was ashamed and embarrassed to read the quotations from our report (paragraphs 3.24 and 3.26, pages 64–5) where we claim that our new and extremely cumbersome terminology would avoid 'stigmatization'. Of course it would not. We were trying to get away from the medical model of referring to 'handicapped' children by reference to what was wrong with them. We wanted to concentrate instead on what they would need if they were to make educational progress. But both our designation of the whole class of such children as 'having special educational needs', and our attempts to describe the kinds of needs that they had and that must be met, (which, with incredible naivety, we alleged would be 'used for descriptive purposes and not for any purpose of categorization') were doomed to failure. Predictably, our designations got shortened into initials (BESD, for example), which then came to be used adjectivally. Once adjectives, they were then used as labels, just as surely as 'maladjusted' or 'mentally subnormal' had been so used before. Even the initials SEN themselves became an adjective with which one nasty child could taunt another. Moreover official handouts and codes of practice fell into total grammatical and conceptual confusion about the difference between names of disabilities and names of needs, so that you would get a list headed 'special needs' followed by a list of things wrong with the child such as dyslexia or Asperger's Syndrome, thus negating the intentions of the original 1978 report.

I understand why we embarked on this exercise, but we should have known that it would not work. There is a lot to be said for going back to the old ways of speaking. It always seems to me to be absurd to speak of a grown-up man who, say, has been mugged in the street as someone with 'learning difficulties'. He was not trying to learn anything when he fell victim to his assailant. But even I would hesitate to refer to him as 'mentally subnormal', though that far more exactly says what is meant. However, we are probably stuck, for the time being, with what we have got. To avoid labelling the whole vocabulary of disability would have to be totally revised every five years or so. And in any case this is probably the least important issue before us, as we contemplate the problems of future provision.

To return: do we still need the overarching category of SEN? As usual, a number of different issues interlock as we try to answer this question. But first there is one general observation that I must make. In the pamphlet I bemoaned the fact that policy-makers tended to lump all SEN children together, as though what would meet the needs of one child would meet the needs of all SEN children. But this is really part of a wider problem. It seems to me that policy-makers, ministers and their civil servants, as well as the vocal disabled lobby, are often forgetful of those children who are most severely disabled, children who are probably going to die in childhood, and who are nevertheless, since 1972, legally entitled to education, and who may enormously benefit from it, as long as their short life lasts. For these children at least, it is essential that special schools should remain open, and should improve, with specialist teachers, medical staff and special equipment at hand all the hours that they are open. And this is happening. There is an increasing number of excellent special schools, both maintained and private, that cater for the severe end of the disability spectrum.

They must be given encouragement (and indeed they are. Ofsted has been said to be embarrassed by how many are classified outstanding) and encouraged not only to keep records of each child's progress, (or, often, not progress but stabilization) but also to make full use of these data for research that can be published.

The sad death in 2009 of six-year-old Ivan Cameron has perhaps opened people's eyes to just how terribly disabled a child can be, what he can suffer, and yet how much his life can be improved if he both goes to a good special school and is lovingly cared for at home. Such children as he certainly have special needs, and among these needs is the need for education. With infinite patience some such children can be taught, for example, what it means to signify by non-verbal means which of two toys they prefer, to smile when they get the one they want, to make eye contact with their teacher. For an immobile, non-speaking child, such advances are enormous, the first step to freedom, and to becoming a person of character. It would be futile to pretend that such children could benefit by being in a mainstream school. No ordinary school could meet their needs.

It is often argued that a special school on a campus shared with a mainstream school is the best solution for educating the severely disabled, and I agree that it can have advantages, at least insofar as other children may benefit from there being a school nurse at hand or there being equipment designed for primary school children available for those of secondary age, if they need it. But if special schools for the severely disabled do share a campus, or even share a building, it is of crucial importance that the funding for the special school is not surreptitiously used for the main school, and that facilities for the special school are not diminished because of the needs of the other school, the meeting of which may bring more obvious glory to the school. The schools must be thought of as separate, even if they are geographically together. With the children I am now considering, there will be no realistic social mixing. I do not accept the argument that it is good for mainstream children to become aware of the existence of such severely disabled children and that they will learn to treat them as equals. It may be so, but they are not going to share any spontaneous social activities with them, and I profoundly dislike the idea of these entirely helpless children being used as a kind of living teaching aid.

So those who advocate the closure of all special schools should be constantly mindful of the fact that it is only in a special environment that the most profoundly disabled can get any education at all. Not every mainstream school can be expected to provide either the expert teachers or the equipment and facilities that they need. I sometimes remember with alarm a visit I, with other member of the Committee of Inquiry, made to Norway in the mid 1970s. Norway was already famous for its policy of integration. There was, for each neighbourhood, including each division of Oslo, just one neighbourhood school and we were shown with pride a number of classes of about 25 children among whom would be three or four Down's Syndrome children or children who were deaf or blind or in wheelchairs. There was, for that time, wonderfully sophisticated portable equipment for the deaf and the blind. In charge of the class there would be one main teacher, who would have a qualification in special education as well as her general teaching degree, and she would have two or three assistants, also trained. Some children had their own specially allocated support teacher. It seemed clear from our observation and our discussions that children with moderate learning difficulties, including many of those with Down's Syndrome, flourished in this environment. I worried, all the same, that we saw no very academically demanding subjects being taught, nor were we taken to any classes for children over the age of about 13. Nevertheless, within these limitations, the belief that all children were really the same was almost palpable. But the more serious aspect of our visit dawned on me only gradually. I realized that we had seen no really severely disabled children. So I asked our mentor from the Local Authority how this came about and she, looking embarrassed, said that they were mostly in hospital. So I said might we, then, visit a hospital school. To which she replied that there were no hospital schools. In fact, though the policy of integration had manifest benefits as far as it went, in other ways Norway was in the legislative position that we were in before 1972, and were just struggling out of, where children with the most severe, multiple and complex disabilities were not entitled to any education at all. I fear that if the abolitionists had their way and all special schools were closed we might drift back to hiding these children away or at least to depriving them of the highly specialized provision that they above all need. This must not be allowed to happen, and the dogmatic special school closure lobby must recognize that for some children special schools are the best or indeed the only option.

But that the most severely disabled need special schools, whether or not co-located with mainstream schools, and whether called schools or units, has no direct relevance to the question whether the overarching category of SEN is any longer needed. We could describe the children I have been talking about as having special educational needs if we liked, just to emphasize the fact that, among their many special needs, education must feature as one. But we could drop the term for all the other children who need more or less additional support temporary or permanent, through their school life, that is for the vast majority of those who now fall under the overarching description of SEN. The severely disabled could be issued with a statement declaring that they had special educational needs and must go to a special school. Keeping the term SEN for this smaller class of children would differentiate this scheme from the Scottish scheme which no longer employs the concept of SEN. But if it remained the case that a Local Authority had a statutory duty to provide only for those children with statements of SEN, then this would leave very large numbers of children at risk of receiving inadequate support, or none at all. In Scotland, after all, Local Authorities have a statutory duty to provide additional support for all who need it, and who must be identified without the use of the concept of special need. To identify the class of those with statements with the class of those designated as having special needs and to confine this class to the most severely disabled would be different from the position I adopted in my pamphlet (pages 38–9). For then I rather briefly advocated the opening of new special schools for children who, while not the most severely disabled, have nevertheless failed to flourish in a mainstream school or whose educational needs are not being fully met in the mainstream, and who would have to have a statement in order to be admitted to a special school. These might include children with emotional and behavioural difficulties, or those with Asperger's Syndrome, or those with sensory deprivation. (It should be remembered how many blind children, for example, have extremely limited access to text books and other written material if they are confined to the resources of the ordinary mainstream school.) I still believe that this is the best solution, and it was a solution apparently favoured by the government in their 2006 White Paper 'Higher Standards, Better Schools for All' (paragraphs 4.19 and 4.20). There they propose new specialist schools, whose specialism should be either SEN or SEN combined with a subject specialism, such as IT or drama or sport. (But I rather fear that this opening up of special schools may have been dear to the heart of the then Parliamentary Under-Secretary, Andrew Adonis, and may have been neglected since he moved on to Transport.)

Linking statements to special schools for a small class of children, those with the most acute educational needs, might allow these children and these schools to be intelligibly referred to, and funded, as a group but it would say nothing about what happens to children, less severely disabled, who remain in mainstream schools. It would say nothing about whether any such children should be designated as having special educational needs. Schools could, as they do now, identify those children who needed additional support by the steps set out in earlier legislation, passing from minor or temporary support to be provided within the school to support that requires provision from outside school. However, I doubt whether it would be easy to carry out such progressive identification of need and to justify the funding of support provision without some terminology or other peculiar to the children in question. It is the dilemma of difference again. To say that these children need more or less additional support is, like it or not, to differentiate them from their fellow pupils, and perhaps it does not very much matter how we refer to them, as long as the designation is not allowed to become positively offensive. And there are, as I have suggested above, many schools where children who require support will be in the majority. In such schools it is perhaps those who find education relatively agreeable who will be 'labelled', or picked out as different. Whatever vocabulary we use, there are going to be parents who are dissatisfied with the assessment of their child and with the support he gets to enable him to make progress, or at least to be happy at school. Part of the task of any new Committee of Inquiry or Commission that was set up would be to examine this dissatisfaction, to what extent it is a matter of funding, to what a matter of the concepts and terminology used at the margins.

If we decide to retain the vocabulary of statements and special educational needs (or if we think it is not a great matter of decision but simply one of convenience) then, however many special schools there are, every student attending a special school should have a statement of educational need, but they would not, as they are not now, be the only children with special educational needs; and it could be argued that, in order to ensure adequate provision for these others, they too should have statements. After all, one of the iniquities of the current system, as I said in the pamphlet, is that some children's needs merit a statement while those of others do not. It could therefore be argued that both those in special schools and those who can be supported successfully in the mainstream should have statements setting out their needs and how they are to be met. This would entail that the term special educational needs or some equivalent term would be retained, but it would now cover all and only those with statements. Thus the number of statements issued would increase, not decrease, since those children who are at present assessed as having special educational needs but are not issued with a statement would also be included. But this seems to me an intolerable conclusion, given the expense, delays and disputes that surround the issuing of statements. However many or few statements were issued, there would remain, as I have said, areas of dispute at the edges, and the more statements there were the greater the number of dissatisfied parents there would be.

I therefore turn with relief to Brahm Norwich's two-tiered system (page 98), which seems to me both ingenious and workable, though it is of course based on the assumption that mainstream schools take seriously the individual educational plans to be drawn up for their students, and that they are absolutely scrupulous about monitoring the students' progress under the plan. That parents would have the option of demanding an assessment for a statement if progress under the plan is not apparent seems to me a great strength of the strategy. I sincerely hope that this is the option that will be adopted.

I must now turn to an issue which is central to the pamphlet but to which I did not do justice. This is the change from the idea of integration, as I explained it above, to that of inclusion. Brahm Norwich, in an endnote (page 110), raises the question of whether I am ambivalent about inclusion as a social as well as an educational value. The answer is that I am indeed doubtful about it as a social value, at least if it is elevated above all others, but that I am a great deal more doubtful about it as an educational value.

William Evans, in his essay 'Reforming Special Educational Needs Law' (Evans, 2007: pages 85–94) points out that special education legislation was for 20 years, from 1981 until 2001, based on the idea of pupils' needs. It was indeed the last legislation to retain this idea from the revolutionary laws of the 1940s that inaugurated the welfare state. This legislation sought to ensure that the needs of citizens, social, health-related or educational, should be met by the state. The 1981 Act can be regarded as the last gasp of welfarism. As Evans puts it 'While the concepts and vocabulary of SEN have remained static since 1981, the vocabulary of disability, like its politics, has moved on. SEN law…. has not kept up; it has fallen behind its peers' (Evans, 2007: page 87). In 2001, the government attempted to remedy this 'falling behind' by marrying SEN legislation to disability legislation, based as that was on the idea of disability discrimination, or the right of disabled people not to suffer discrimination or be treated worse than others on grounds of their disability alone. In the 2001 Special Educational Needs and Disability Act the definition of disability was taken over from the earlier Disability Discrimination Act, namely that a person is disabled if he or she has 'a physical or mental impairment that has a substantial and long-term adverse effect on his or her ability to carry our normal day-to-day activities'. The drawback in suddenly adding on the concept of disability discrimination to the existing education acts, without introducing a new definition of disability, is that the old definition really has nothing to do with education. Provided that a school adapted by putting in ramps or handrails, a student with mobility impairment might have no special educational needs, but might perhaps sue the school for discrimination if she was excluded from taking part in a school rock-climbing expedition or given no chance to take part in sports. It was from this forced marriage of SEN with disability discrimination that the notion of inclusion was born. Inclusion is essentially connected with citizens' rights, not needs. It is thus an overtly political concept. To infringe a person's rights is to exclude him or her from a proper membership of society. William Evans suggests (2007, page 88) that one way out of the difficulty would be to repeal SEN law altogether, as a distinct area of public law, and to extend the concept of disability to include learning difficulties, of whatever kind. Many difficulties would remain with regard to provision. But what parents, Local Authorities and schools would have to determine would be whether the pupil in question was or was not a disabled person and, if so, whether the school had made reasonable adjustments as required by disability discrimination law. Then at least the idea of inclusion would be firmly based on current laws and values, even if the decisions to be made about individual pupils might be no less contentious than they are now. Brahm Norwich's fifth option for the future (page 99) is a refined version of what Evans suggests as a possibility.

I can see that such proposals as these would bring considerably greater coherence to the law, and this would be an advantage. As I said at the beginning of this response, it is genuinely unclear, as things stand, what the duties of individual schools and Local Authorities are, and in what circumstances either might be sued for unlawful discrimination. Though now the words 'special educational needs' and 'disability' sit side by side in the title of the 2001 Act, there has been no effort to explain how the two concepts are related, nor does the Act contain any statement of general principle as its first clause. It is in fact a thoroughly bad piece of legislation, and I would love to see it repealed.

However, it will come as no surprise that I would not support any move to bring all legislation relating to the education of children with learning disabilities under the umbrella of anti-discrimination. I believe that whatever vocabulary we adopt to deal with special education, legislation that covers it must be kept separate from general discrimination law. The reason is simple: in society as a whole, laws against discrimination are concerned to ensure that members of a society are treated justly with respect to the provision of goods, services and benefits that society should bring. All members of the society should be included, in the sense that all should have the same rights and entitlements. No one should be excluded from the goods that are on offer on the grounds that he is a Jew, say, or a homosexual, that he is black, or a Roman Catholic. Anti-discrimination legislation reflects an ideal of society in which everyone is equal, subject to the same laws, but equally enabled to benefit from them.

All such legislation is contentious and often difficult either to formulate or to put into practice, as we see from attempts legally to exclude those suspected of inciting people to terrorism from the exercise of what are generally supposed to be their rights. None is more difficult than disability discrimination. In the matter of job applications, for example, no amount of adaptation on an employer's part could make it feasible for someone in a wheelchair to apply successfully for a job as a scaffolder; and if he did apply and his application was rejected, he could not possibly claim that his right to equal treatment had been infringed. His disability in this case was strictly relevant to the nature of the job. In my view at least, those disabled people who claim that disabilities are simply social constructs, that no one would be disabled if society did not make them so, are blinding themselves to the truth. If someone has had his legs amputated, he cannot be a scaffolder; if someone is blind, he cannot man a lookout post; if he is deaf, he cannot successfully sit as a judge or conduct an orchestra. Nevertheless, even though some people may be intrinsically unfitted for some employment, in the workplace anti-discrimination legislation is over all good, and brings us nearer to the ideal of justice that is at its heart. Disabilities that are irrelevant to a job should be treated as irrelevant, and, as the law demands, if someone's job is made more difficult by his disability (as a wheelchair-user who is a teacher might find it difficult to get from one part of the school to another) then as far as possible the school should adapt to his needs, so that his disability becomes irrelevant to his job. And of course with regard to matters such as salary and entitlement to holidays or pension, his disability is already irrelevant.

Even within society as a whole, however, I believe, as Brahm Norwich detects, that the ideal of inclusion can be carried too far, if it leads to the conclusion that no group in society should be 'exclusive'. The trouble is that words such as 'exclusive' or 'elite' are habitually used as derogatory terms or as carrying a connotation of injustice. But no one can doubt that society would be the poorer if there were no groups of its members that were relatively small and exclusive. I am thinking of such groups as those of pure mathematicians or instrumental musicians, brain surgeons or jockeys. The question of justice comes in only if people are prevented from even trying to be members of a particular group. A deaf person can try and even, amazingly, succeed in being a great percussionist. But the principle that no one should do what not everyone can do is surely disastrous. This is why, even speaking of political ideals or ideals of civil society, I prefer the word 'integration' to 'inclusion'. As I said above it suggests, to me at least, people who have different tastes, different ambitions, different beliefs and cultures nevertheless settling down and interlocking with one another, rather than sharing all their goals and interests.

In any case, this aspect of the value of inclusion is an irrelevant consideration, which should not have appeared even fleetingly in the pamphlet. For it was and remains my contention that schools cannot be treated as microcosms of society. What can be said of the political aims of society cannot necessarily be said of schools which are not, or should not be, political bodies. Schools have one common ambition, to civilize and educate their pupils; they are devoted to one enterprise which is teaching and learning. I know that children must learn not only academic subjects, but how to behave, how to interact and communicate with other people, how to overcome setbacks and solve problems. This kind of learning is often referred to as a preparation for life, and it is therefore assumed that the more a school mirrors the society into which a child will eventually emerge, the better this preparation will be. It is therefore better, so the argument goes, that a child should share his classroom with those who are different from himself, for this is how he will live in the outside world. I do not claim that there is nothing in this argument, but I am not persuaded by it, especially where secondary schools are concerned. I would simply reiterate my arguments in favour of small schools, whether special schools or hybrid schools, as Norwich I think suggests. It is the size that matters. I certainly know of a hybrid school for deaf and hearing children, where all the language-based subjects are taught to the deaf children, at least in the early years, by specialist teachers of the deaf, but all other activities are fully integrated, and where many of the hearing children choose to learn sign language to communicate with their deaf fellows. Such a hybrid school certainly has many advantages, provided that the hearing and the deaf children really know and respect each other, and each has the interests of the others at heart.

There could be many other models. After all what many special (or special and specialist) schools have in common is that, for whatever reason, many of their pupils have had bad experiences at mainstream schools. They may have been terrorized by the size and pace of secondary school after managing quite well before they left their primary schools. Their dyslexia, for example, may have become an overwhelming problem only when the secondary curriculum made demands that they could no longer conceal. Their Asperger's characteristics may have made their difference from other children more conspicuous with adolescence. Bad experience may have led to their being excluded or to their simply leaving, or being removed by their parents. Such children who know their own vulnerabilities may flourish at a school where all the staff, teaching, administrative and domestic, are united in aiming for the good of the children in the school with whose difficulties they are personally acquainted. Such a school is exactly the kind of institution that will develop its own ethos and its own pride. It will be an institution within which all the members can take pride. Such a school is of course cosy, and it is undoubtedly cosier that either a large comprehensive school or what society at large may prove to be for most of the pupils who attend it. Some of the pupils may miss it when they leave, but many will by then be stronger than they were when they arrived and be ready to move on, whether back to a large school, or to the next stage of their life. There are two more points I would make. I think Brahm Norwich is far too optimistic when he says that there are other ways to combat bullying than sending victims (or perpetrators indeed) to special schools. It is doubtless true that some schools, where the teachers are good and the head is influential in creating an ethos of caring about other people, may devise a 'whole school policy' that works. This is far easier when a large proportion of the pupils come from homes where bullying is also disapproved of. But pupils at school are not yet grown-up. They have to be taught how to behave to one another, and how to resist the temptation of bullying those whom they see to be weaker than themselves. It is a matter of constant vigilance, and this is not always possible. A child may be bulled as much on the bus ride to school as in the corridors of the school itself. Moreover, what may seem to some like legitimate teasing may appear as torture to the child who, for whatever reason, is lacking in confidence and cannot laugh it off. Asperger's Syndrome children are especially prey to this kind of jokey banter, since for them there really are no jokes.

My second and final point is this. The Special Educational Needs and Discrimination Act 2001 has, albeit somewhat uncertainly, made it an infringement of a child's rights if he is refused a place at a mainstream school on account of his disability. It is probably an assumption of the Act that if a child is so profoundly disabled that the school would have to change its whole character and all its budgeting, equipment and staffing, even geographical layout to accommodate him, he may legitimately be refused entry. Such changes would not be reasonable adaptation. And in practice this is probably accepted by most parents, who will prefer a special school for such a severely disabled child, knowing that expert teachers are essential if he is to progress even a little. But it is not hard to imagine a parent of such a child who is also a strict believer in the phasing out of special schools, a fundamentalist with regard to abolition. That parent will argue that it is every child's right to be educated in the mainstream, and I have heard many disabled people say this. The 2001 Act, as I have argued, is bad law because on this precise issue it is less than clear. It seems to suggest that it is a child's right to receive his education at a mainstream school, or a parent's right to arrange for him to be so educated, except in certain circumstances. The fundamentalist parent would argue that to make exceptions is to deny the child his rights, as one could argue that freedom of expression is a right, and to deny it to a suspected terrorist is to infringe that right. So the parent might attempt to insist that the school of his choice make the adaptations necessary to receive his child, or at least that some mainstream school within the area do so. The danger about such a dispute is that, if one takes a positivist view of rights, the only certain right that a child has, since 1972, is the right to education. According to that law, there is no stipulation about where he is to be educated. The overriding purpose of the 1981 Education Act was to ensure as far as possible that children received the best education for them, and it was in the passage of this Act that there began to be the presumption in law that the best education would be with his contemporaries in the mainstream. But suppose, as I would maintain, that the best education for a particular child were in a special school, co-located perhaps, or in a unit within a mainstream school, but not itself an all-inclusive mainstream school.

Then, if he were not permitted to attend a special school or unit and if his education would proceed worse unless he did attend such a school or unit, would it not be arguable that his original right, the right to education, would be infringed? Abolitionists, total inclusionists, simply answer this question by saying that every child has the right to a place at the same school as the rest. They do not face the question of whether the point of the 1972 Act was to get for every child the best possible education for him. It is as if the only right a child had was to go to a mainstream school, regardless of the outcome. There is really no arguing against such a fundamentalist position. It is a matter of faith.

What we really need is evidence of where different children with different disabilities thrive best, and how the pitiful casualties of some inclusive comprehensive schools can be best avoided. Everyone in the field is demanding evidence, and efforts are being made to provide it. One advantage of retaining the overarching collective category of SEN is that a stronger duty could be laid on teachers of children with special needs, wherever they are being educated, and on SENCOs to keep detailed records of progress and to use these records so that comparative research within different clusters of schools could be made available for research, and wider evidence-based comparative studies could be carried out. Comparisons would be difficult, and great care would need to be taken to avoid extrapolating from one kind of disability to another. But without evidence it is to be feared that the arguments will remain as dogmatic and intuitive as they are at present, which would be to nobody's advantage, least of all the children who are the subject of this debate.

Note

6   The Lamb Inquiry was published on 16 December 2009, while this book was in preparation. The authors cannot therefore comment on it, nor on the response from the government. However, it is perhaps worth saying that this book deals with general issues, which are not addressed in the Report. For instance, the Report does not support a reviewing

of the concept of special educational needs, as this is seen 'to divert energies away from more fundamental changes we seek to bring about in behaviour, attitudes and in the priority given to outcomes for disabled children and children with SEN.' Section 6.36.

References

Audit Commission (2002), *Statutory Assessment and Statements: in Need of Review?*. London: Audit Commission.

Audit Commission (2002), *Special Educational Needs: A Mainstream Issue*. London: Audit Commission.

DCSF, (2009) *Lamb Inquiry: Special Educational Needs and Parental Confidence*. London: DCSF, available at www.dcsf.gov.uk

Department for Children, Families and Schools (2006), *Higher Standards, Better Schools for All*. London: Stationery Office.

Department of Education and Science (1978), *Special Educational Needs* (The Warnock Report). London: HMSO.

Department for Education and Skills (2004), *14–19 Curriculum and Qualifications Reform: Final Report of the Working Group on 14–19 Reform* (The Tomlinson Report). Annesley: DfES Publications.

Dyson A. (2001), 'Special Needs in the Twenty-first Century: Where We've Been and Where We're Going', *British Journal of Special Education* vol. 28, no.1, 24–29.

Evans, W. (2007), 'Reforming Special Educational Needs Law: Vocabulary and Distributive Justice' in Cigman, R. (2007), *Included or Excluded? The Challenge of the Mainstream for Some Children with SEN* (ed). London: Routledge.

House of Commons Education and Skills Committee (2006), *Special Educational Needs*. Third Report of Session 2005–06. London: Stationery Office.

House of Commons Education and Skills Committee (2007), *Special Educational Needs: Assessment and Funding*. London: Stationery Office.

Minow, M. (1990), *Making All the Difference: Inclusion, Exclusion and American Law*. Ithaca: Cornell University Press.

Norwich, B. (1996), 'Special Needs Education, Inclusive Education or Just Education for All?' (Inaugural Lecture). Institute of Education, University of London.

Ofsted (2004), *Special Educational Needs and Disability: Towards Inclusive Schools*. London: Audit Commission.

Ofsted (2006), *Inclusion: Does it Matter where Pupils are Taught? Provision and Outcomes in Different Settings for Pupils with Learning Difficulties and Disabilities*. HMI 2535.

Visser, J. and Upton, G. (1993), *Special Education in Britain after Warnock*. London: David Fulton Publishers.

Warnock, M. (2005), *Special Educational Needs: A New Look*. London: Philosophy of Education Society of Great Britain, Impact Series N.11.

Afterword: Difference, equality and the ideal of inclusion in education

Lorella Terzi

Three fundamental questions are central to the contributions in this volume: the concepts used to identify children's differences in learning; the necessity of statements to justify and ensure differential provision; and the value of inclusion, both as social and educational ideal. These questions all involve considerations about the interrelation between theory and practice and, as Warnock reminds us by calling for more evidence to improve the current debate, they also entail insights about the role of evidence-based research in informing theory and practice.

In these concluding notes, I shall address some of the main implications of the positions presented in this volume, in particular with respect to identifying children's disabilities and difficulties in learning, and to the value of inclusion. My analysis will be informed by insights drawn on the capability approach, as developed by economist and philosopher Amartya Sen to address issues of injustice and poverty. As I have argued at length elsewhere, the approach offers important innovative insights on many of the contentious issues at stake in the provision for children with special educational needs (Terzi, 2005, 2008). Two ideas are especially relevant to this debate: the concept of 'capabilities for functionings', i.e. the genuine opportunities that individuals have to choose the kind of life they have reason to value, and the fundamental role of agency in the realization of one's valued plans (Sen, 1992). In particular, the concept of capability for functionings is specifically apt to express children's differences in learning, and provides an alternative framework for re-conceptualizing disability and special educational needs. While the idea of functioning alone makes sense of a disability or a difficulty, the concept of capability for functionings is related to a complex notion of human diversity, including personal and social elements, and suggests a relational conception of difficulties in learning as resulting from the interaction of individual and contextual features. Furthermore, the ideal of capability equality, or equality in genuine opportunities for educational functionings, can add a significant conceptual dimension to the contentious debate on inclusion.

In referring to this approach, my focus in these concluding notes will therefore be intentionally theoretical, but with due consideration of the many contextual factors which play an important role, both in shaping ideas and in their enactment in practice. I shall start by addressing the identification of children's differences, both in terms of needs and capability, and subsequently proceed to analyze the debate about inclusive education.

1. Identifying children's differences in education: needs or capabilities?

In her contribution to this volume, Warnock reminds us of the rationale behind the introduction of the concept of special educational needs, and the advantages it aimed to bring to the education of children identified as experiencing these needs. Underpinning the adoption of the concept of educational needs was the idea of common educational goals considered important for all children, and the shared conviction that emphasis should be placed, not on the difficulties experienced by some children in their learning, but rather on what they would need if they were to make educational progress (page 16), and thus on the kind of additional provision required to achieve the established goals. Warnock further reminds us that the concept of special educational needs aimed at expressing the continuum of ability and disability characterizing children's differences, and hence at bringing about a more positive approach than those previously deployed (page 17). Three main advantages were expected from the introduction of this new 'framework-concept', to adopt Warnock's expression. First, the new concept intended to abolish the use of categories of disability and their associated negative connotations, while going beyond medical views of difficulties in learning. It is perhaps worth mentioning here that, at the time of the publication of the Warnock Report, 11 categories of 'handicap' were in use (Wedell, 2008: page 51). Second, the concept was seen as emphasizing what was positive with children, and hence their abilities and dispositions, rather than focusing only on their difficulties. Finally, the concept was considered important in implementing children's equal entitlement to education, thus emphasizing their sameness, but with due provision for their differences. A positive approach, ultimately, characterized the introduction of the framework of needs in education, and with it, as we have seen, an attempt to address the dilemma of difference.

As Warnock highlights, however, the framework of special educational needs has produced contrasting results, and, in her view, this is a consequence of the superficiality of the Committee's position. Although this retrospective critique by Warnock might appear severe, especially in the light of the positive contributions of the Report, both Warnock and Norwich clearly outline that, in the last two decades, the usefulness of the concept of educational needs has been a source of consistent discussion and research in academic and policy arenas alike. Warnock herself, as we have seen, maintains that the Warnock Committee's attempt to address the dilemma of difference through the framework of special educational needs has, predictably, been unsuccessful. In her view, the main problem of the framework consists in its failed attempt to abolish categories, and also to distinguish between different kinds of needs. The latter problem has, in turn, led to a view of all special educational needs as a unified class of differences (page 13), and thus ultimately to a provision which does not meet the specificity of needs.

However, Norwich argues that Warnock's critique of the concept of special educational needs as unspecified is perhaps not entirely accurate, since the Report recognizes degrees of needs to which differential provision is due (page 60). According to Norwich, the concept of special educational needs has positively contributed to the recognition of children's differences within an educational context, and has led to the important identification of a group of children as vulnerable (page 82). In his view, the main limitations of the framework relate instead and primarily to its attempt to abolish the use of categories in the field, and to its enactment in ways which still identify special educational needs with children's difficulties (page 64). More specifically, Norwich convincingly argues that the concept of special educational needs, rather than abandoning the use of categories, has replaced them as a super-ordinate category (page 64). He furthermore shows how successive specifications of the concept, for example through the implementation of the current Code of Practice (DfE, 2001), have resulted in the conflation of special educational needs with learning difficulties, seen as features inherent to the child, thus completely losing the positive connotations that the original concept entailed (page 84). Norwich mentions, for example, how the category of educational sub-normality, in use prior to the introduction of the concept of special educational needs, has merely been replaced by a new definition of moderate learning difficulties (page 84). He furthermore shows how such difficulties are currently conceptualized primarily in terms of 'child features'.

It is against this background that Norwich suggests a system of identification of differences in learning still based on the conceptual framework of needs, but specifying needs on three dimensions: needs common to all children, needs specific to a group and needs unique to individuals (page 93). Norwich inscribes this system within the bio-psycho-social model of disability which informs the 2007 International Classification of Functioning (ICF) of the World Health Organisation. This model, Norwich maintains, emphasizes the relational nature of any difference or difficulty in learning, seen as resulting from the interaction of biological, psychological and social elements, thus overcoming unilateral and devaluing 'within-child' perspectives. At the same time, as we have seen, Norwich's suggested system is inscribed in a plural values framework, which includes the interaction of the values of equality and respect, in an attempt to give expression to elements of commonality and difference. Norwich further advocates a revised and reduced role for a concept of 'functional difficulty' in education, in the light of the attention placed on individual needs in his multidimensional framework and against its broader recognition of common needs (page 94).

Norwich's analysis of the concept of special educational needs shows very clearly, not only the main positions informing the current debate, but also the difficulties inherent to the idea of special educational needs as a framework-concept. However, notwithstanding the limitations highlighted, Norwich's proposal is based on a further specification of the same needs framework, and perhaps this leaves his suggestion open to some of the difficulties expressed in relation to the concept of special educational needs. More specifically, two problems could still arise from his tri-dimensional identification of educational needs. First is the question of a super-ordinate category. It might be argued that the framework could still reproduce the distinction between children experiencing unique needs and children experiencing only 'common needs', whereby the 'uniqueness of needs' might become a new super-ordinate category. And this problem might still manifest itself even within the significant and carefully outlined plural values system defended by Norwich. Second, and importantly, the three dimensions specified as constitutive of the framework of needs, i.e. common needs, group-based needs and individual unique needs, while being an interesting specification of the concept, might nevertheless give rise to a conceptual proliferation of 'kinds of needs', and therefore require a more specific classification of the needs under each dimension, which could be both theoretically debatable and also problematic to apply in practice. Finally, it could be argued that needs common to a group of children could end up been considered nominally different, but substantially equal, to the current understanding of special educational needs. For example, dyslexia may be seen as a need common to a group, i.e. the group of dyslexic students, who would still require, both individually and as a group, a different kind of provision from that required by students with common needs only, thus somehow reproducing the existing framework. Despite its own merits, therefore, it seems that Norwich's suggestion might encounter at least some problems similar to those it aims to overcome.

The dimensions of the concept of special educational needs outlined so far in relation to Warnock's and Norwich's positions, despite several positive elements, show some conceptual and practical limitations, which suggest that a reconsideration of the whole framework might be necessary and helpful. Indeed, this is partly recognized by both Warnock and Norwich when they address the question of whether it would overall be better to abandon the special educational needs framework, and adopt, for instance, the system of additional needs established in Scotland, or alternative schemes. However, as we have seen, both authors' positions remain ultimately inscribed within the conceptual framework of needs, albeit with some important specifications.

In what follows, I shall outline some elements of a different theoretical framework, based on the capability approach, which can be seen as a promising advancement in the debate. My analysis will specifically address the issues raised about the concept of special educational needs by both authors in this volume. It will include a brief overview of the main themes of the approach and its reframing of concepts of disability and special educational needs, as well as an outline of some of the advantages entailed by the adoption of such a framework.

Originally developed within welfare economics and political philosophy by Amartya Sen (1984, 1992, 1999), and further articulated by Martha Nussbaum (2000, 2006), in the last two decades the capability approach has increasingly influenced academic research as well as policy-making (Robeyns, 2006: page 351). Sen introduced the concept of capability to evaluate individuals' well-being and the justice of social and institutional arrangements. Instead of the amount of goods or services consumed, Sen maintains that individuals' well-being should be assessed in terms of capabilities, i.e. the real opportunities – the real freedoms – that people have to choose and pursue valuable forms of living, or, as Sen says, to achieve valued functionings. Reading, or taking part in the life of the community, or being healthy, are all possible examples of functionings. Sen notably places the concept of human difference at the core of this evaluative framework. He specifies human heterogeneity to include personal, social and contextual factors, as well as cultural and attitudinal elements, together with the crucially important factor of conversion of resources into well-being, which so differs among individuals. As Sen notices in a well-known example to illustrate this factor, due to her different conversion of resources, a lactating woman requires more food for her functioning than a non-lactating one (Sen, 1992). Furthermore, Sen emphasizes the important role of agency in leading a worthwhile life, where agency is seen as the freedom to bring about one's considered valuable achievements. Thus, according to Sen, the justice of a specific social arrangement or the comparative evaluation of individuals' reciprocal positions should be based on a metric of capabilities, or the opportunities for functionings that people have. Applied to education, this view implies placing the notion of well-being at the centre of the educational process and securing equal levels of real opportunities for educational functionings (such as reading and writing, for example).

How can the capability approach be used to identify and describe children's differences and difficulties in learning? And furthermore, how can such a framework help in addressing some of the limitations outlined with respect to the concept of special educational needs?

Several conceptual aspects, pertaining both to the concept of capability and to the ethical nature of the approach, can inform the debate on these issues. First, there is a conceptual gain in adopting the idea of capability. This consists in a relational definition of learning difficulties and disability in terms of limitation of capability, which goes beyond unilateral individual or social causal explanations, and is furthermore seen as an aspect of human diversity among all the others (Terzi, 2005, 2008). More specifically, the concept of functionings accounts for the possible restrictions relating to impairment, while the idea of capability expresses the consequent limitations in opportunities for functionings pertaining to disability. Since an individual's functioning, and therefore his or her functional difficulty, depends on the interrelation of individual, social and contextual factors, the nature of the capability limitation is neither individually nor socially determined, but it is seen as a result of such interrelation of factors. Both personal characteristics and the design of social and institutional arrangements are therefore important in determining whether an individual impairment results in functional difficulties or restrictions, and therefore in a limitation of capabilities. Moreover, the framework of capability does not entail the use of specific categories, but rather focuses on possible functionings, however common or atypical they might be, as expression of human diversity. This is important in working towards a framework which avoids devaluing individuals, and particularly in relation to individuals who have experienced discrimination as a result of their particular differences. To illustrate the reach of this re-conceptualization, consider for instance the case of dyslexia. The learning difficulty of a student with dyslexia can be seen as a limitation in functionings (reading and writing functionings) resulting from the interaction of the personal characteristics of the child with the schooling environment (especially in systems where literacy is central). Where the latter is not appropriately designed, and/or the individual is not receptive to it, then the functional restriction amounts to a limitation of capabilities, thus to a limitation of the opportunities, present and future, that the child has. Here the emphasis is not placed on individual or on social causes, but truly focuses on their interconnection. Finally, the functional restriction is inscribed in a broad framework where, to reiterate what I said above, atypical functionings and more typical ones are equally considered (Terzi, 2005, 2008, 2009).

Second, the capability approach gives expression to the agency of individuals as fundamental in leading good lives, an element less emphasized by the idea of needs, although not absent from, or inconsistent with it (Alkire, 2005). The emphasis on agency is important in overcoming some forms of presumed passivity, or negative and patronizing images of 'neediness', which, as Norwich reminds us (page 85), have been associated with the concept of special educational needs by some of its critics (whether rightly or wrongly is beyond my analysis in these notes). Finally, the concept of capability is inscribed in a unified ethical framework whose dimensions of equality and its importance for well-being can positively inform and transform the current educational system. Placing the well-being of students with disabilities and special educational needs at the centre of the educational process, while considering the expansion of their capabilities for functionings and their agency suggests a shift from narrowly defined educational outcomes, for instance in terms of academic achievement only, to broader aims including social, relational and participatory elements.

However, some might argue that the same critiques raised in relation to the concept of special educational needs, as well as in relation to Norwich's dimensions of needs, could be made to the capability approach as applied to disability and learning difficulties. After all, while a potential proliferation of kinds of functionings is avoided, since functionings are indeed countless but certainly identifiable as typical or atypical, one might still object that restrictions in functionings and related capabilities, or indeed atypical functionings, could become an overarching category in themselves. In my view, although this may well be so, the ethical nature of the concept of capability, and its specific understanding of human diversity encompassing all functionings on an equal basis, whether typical or atypical, count as positive elements in preventing such a use. Furthermore, the framework of capability might go in the direction advocated by Norwich when he says that 'a new formulation of functional difficulty in educational terms would enable a more explicit use of a "response to teaching" model' (page 94), thus enhancing the educational experience and overall provision for children.

But there are further advantages that can be obtained in adopting this ethical framework. First, the concept of capability for functionings, while being inscribed in a unified ethical perspective, goes beyond the problematic distinction between the concept of disability and that of special educational needs which characterizes the current system, and in particular recent legislation, such as the 2001 Special Educational Needs and Disability Act. This responds to some of Warnock's concerns about this specific law and its enactment. Second, such a framework, if successfully implemented, could overcome the present inconsistencies in the ways in which special educational needs are defined and identified. And although the implementation of such a framework would require extensive further analysis, examples of capability indicators are currently used to inform worldwide projects in various fields, such as development economics and health, as well as projects to address social inequalities in England (Burchardt and Vizard, 2007). Thus the approach appears feasible to be implemented in practice. Third, the approach is certainly well suited, given its attention to social and cultural inequalities, to consider those restrictions that arise from social deprivation which are not addressed by the framework of educational needs, thus responding to some of Warnock's concerns expressed in this volume. Finally, whether the capability framework would require a process of statement is to be ascertained in relation to the policy specifications of such an idea – an area which requires however further elaboration.

All things considered, therefore, it seems that the capability approach does allow for important conceptual, ethical and, possibly, practical gains in relation to many of the problematic aspects of the concept of special educational needs so cogently debated in this volume by Warnock and Norwich. I now turn my attention to the discussion of questions of inclusion in education.

2. Inclusion, inclusive education and capability equality

Interrelated to the political notion of social exclusion (Sen, 2000; Jayal, 2009), the ideas of inclusion and inclusive education are relatively recent, yet highly debated. While the concept of inclusion has been used in the last 30 years in the European Union and the UK to qualify various political attempts to include those at the margins of society (Jayal, 2009: page 363), the idea of inclusive education has mainly been defined in terms of educating children with special educational needs in mainstream schools, thus including them in a system from which they were previously excluded. However, the relation between social and educational inclusion, as well as the precise definition and the value of inclusive education are rather contentious (Pirrie and Head, 2007). Both Warnock and Norwich acknowledge this complexity in their contributions to this volume and highlight the debated nature of the ideal, with particular attention to its enactment in education. As we have seen, however, the two authors differ consistently on the value of the ideal and its significance for education. While Warnock considers inclusion a questionable principle, both socially and, even more so, educationally, Norwich recognizes its importance for society, and supports the idea of educating children in common school, albeit within a specified framework of provision. Indeed, it is precisely on the ideal of inclusive education that the authors diverge more substantially than on any other question they analyze in this volume. It is therefore important to revisit their discussion, and to highlight the terms of the debate, with a view to subsequently considering whether the capability approach and, more specifically, the ideal of capability equality in education, might provide some insights on the questions at stake.

As we have seen, Warnock is highly critical of what she defines the political 'ideology of inclusion' (page 13), and particularly its application to the context of education. According to Warnock, while the ideal of social inclusion 'springs from hearts in the right place' (page 33), i.e. from a commitment to justice and equality of opportunity, as well as to ideas such as accessibility and widening participation, its elevation above all other values, and its extension to all sections of society is, in her opinion, 'surely disastrous' (page 135). Warnock qualifies social inclusion as the principle 'that no one should do what not everyone can do' (page 135), and expresses her profound reservation on the applicability of this principle to all aspects of social life. Two main examples are used to support her critical stance: the first pertains to the arts (page 33), and the second to membership of specific groups, such as the pure mathematicians or the brain surgeons (page 135). Warnock maintains that 'in the context of the arts, for example, inclusiveness dictates that no art form should be encouraged, let alone subsidized, that is not popular, already demanded by the public or enjoyed by a majority' (page 33). No forms of artistic expertise or discernment are allowed, she continues, since this is considered elitist, and therefore exclusionary. Warnock expresses the same idea in her second example, namely access to positions such as the study and practice of pure mathematics and the exercise of highly specialized forms of medicine, such as brain surgery, which require expertise and excellence in a wide range of knowledge, skills and attitudes (page 135). Warnock is here particularly critical of an extensive application of the ideal of social inclusion, if this leads to the conclusion that membership of these specific groups should not be limited or, more generally, that no group in society should be exclusive (page 135). What seems to underpin her stance is a concern for excellence and the preservation of valued forms of civic and social engagement. Warnock is also critical of the common derogatory connotations associated with terms such as 'exclusive' and 'elitist', often seen as expressing forms of injustice, and maintains instead that 'no one can doubt that society would be poorer if there were no groups of its members that were relatively small and exclusive... The question of justice comes in only if people are prevented from even trying to be members of a particular group' (page 135). It is on the bases of these critical insights, as we have seen, that Warnock defends a notion of social integration as a more feasible value than social inclusion. Integration, in her view, amounts to 'people who have different tastes, different ambitions, different beliefs and cultures nevertheless settling down and interlocking with one another, rather than sharing all their goals and interests' (page 135).

But, as we have seen, Warnock is even more critical about the ideal of inclusion applied to education and, in particular to the education of children with special educational needs. She reminds us of the Committee's original endorsement of the integration of children with special educational needs into mainstream schools as 'the possibility of children who were different from one another living peacefully beside those to whom they were different, their differences recognized' (page 125). However, while in her view some reservation can be expressed for the idea of educational integration, for example in the case of children with severe and complex disabilities, Warnock argues that the introduction of the concept of inclusion – seen as the idea that all children should be educated in the mainstream – is certainly highly questionable, if not completely disastrous. As Norwich notices (page 74), Warnock makes two fundamental points in relation to inclusive education. The first is a critique of the ideal specified in terms of educating all children 'under the same roof' (page 101), and the second relates to the view that schools should not be seen as 'microcosms' of society (page 136), but as particular institutions whose enterprise is learning and teaching, and thus preparing children for life, without necessarily or entirely reflecting societal structures and values (page 136). In Warnock's view, furthermore, the critique of inclusive education is interrelated to the value and the role accorded to special schools within the broader schooling system. But let us address these critical stances more closely.

Warnock's concerns in relation to the education of all children 'under the same roof' are primarily based on evaluations of the reality of mainstream schooling for many children with special educational needs, and particularly for those with severe needs and disabilities, who require specialized support, and for children with behavioural and emotional needs, as well as those with autism. Evidence shows that for all these children, Warnock argues, mainstream education, and specifically secondary mainstream education, is often a very negative experience, and one that can affect and hinder their entire lives (page 30). Given that many children with special educational needs are de facto denied an appropriate education in the mainstream, Warnock continues, the ideal of inclusive education as education 'under one roof' should be reconsidered, together with the policy towards further inclusion, and the related decreased role for special schools advocated by the current government (page 29). Warnock's second critique of inclusive education relates to the role of schools within society. According to Warnock, the argument that schools should reflect the diversity of society, and thus include all children in one common school, is not convincing. Schools, Warnock maintains, are not political institutions or microcosms of society (page 136), but rather institutions that should focus on learning and teaching. And while learning includes also aspects of socialization and interaction with others, a kind of preparation for life, it is questionable that such learning should take place in common classes which reflect the diversity of society. In her view, this is particularly the case when these settings are not providing a good level of education and a positive experience for vulnerable children. As Norwich notices, Warnock does not specifically argue her point about the relation between schools and society, but rather reinstates at this stage her recommendation for small specialist or special schools, including hybrid solutions, where commonality and differentiated learning can take place. And certainly a political view of education would find Warnock's position questionable (see, for example, Gutmann, 1987).

On the bases of these critical stances, Warnock suggests a conception of inclusive education defined as the commonality in the enterprise of learning, wherever one can learn best. We should be concerned, Warnock claims, not with the right of all children to be educated together, since this is manifestly unattainable for some, but rather with their right to receive an appropriate education. And for some of the most vulnerable children this right, in her view, is best enacted through small, specialist schools, where resources, expertise, and dedicated staff can enable these children to feel secure and confident, thus facilitating their learning. The concept of inclusive education, ultimately, is redefined by Warnock in terms of the involvement in the common enterprise of learning, rather than in terms of learning in common schools.

As we have seen, Norwich disagrees with Warnock, and raises several questions about her perspective, pertaining mainly to her interpretation of the value of inclusive education. Norwich rightly acknowledges a certain confusion characterizing current definitions and usages of the concept of inclusion in education (page 100), and points to the abstract and multifaceted nature of the concept, which makes it hard 'to apply it in everyday policy and practice' (page 100). While highlighting that Warnock's position on the matter is quite clear (page 100), he nevertheless critiques it by questioning whether her stance is not altogether to be considered 'a closing down on a separatist position' (page 74), without full evaluation of all aspects of the argument. More specifically, Norwich questions Warnock's stance against educating all children 'under one roof', and her claim about the separation of schooling and society. As he notices in relation to the first point, emphasizing only the placement aspect of inclusive education neglects the fact that such education can accommodate the element of placement, together with those of curriculum and learning experience, through appropriate settings and policies (page 74). In rejecting the idea of the common school as unfeasible, Norwich continues, Warnock opts for one aspect of schools, i.e. the aspect of placement, over all the others, thus neglecting how this can be successfully combined with broader elements, such as curricular and methodological ones. In addition, and related to Warnock's position about schools and society, Norwich emphasizes that inclusive schools provide also a common social context, and thus the social learning associated with participating in it (page 76). This aspect, which is highly valued by many educationalists for its importance for children and for society, is completely overlooked by Warnock. Moreover, Norwich notices that Warnock's conception of inclusive education as the common enterprise of learning can be extended to the direct participation in common schools, when these are appropriately designed (page 81), and is therefore not incompatible with the common school ideal. In his words, 'it could be argued that common educational goals call for schools to be places for the social experience of and interaction with different children and young people, including those with disabilities and difficulties' (page 77). Norwich further supports his critique of Warnock's position on inclusive education by referring to research evidence. He maintains that the shortcomings in the current educational system, in cases when inclusion is not successful, as denounced by Warnock, more than the failure of the ideal, reflect 'the quality of general provision' (page 74), and therefore 'can be a useful source of school improvement strategy' (page 74). Finally, according to Norwich, 'review of empirical studies relevant to the outcomes of inclusive education over the last two decades have not been conclusive' (page 75), thus suggesting that the reality of inclusion in education might be more complex, and overall perhaps not as negative as Warnock evaluates it.

In the light of these arguments, Norwich supports and outlines a perspective on inclusion based on a complex interrelation of the values of respect for individual differences and of equality and common provision. In his perspective, the dilemma at the core of provision for children with special educational needs, i.e. whether to emphasize individuality and difference or to accentuate sameness and equality, and the related uncertainties and possible contradictions of current policies, can be resolved only when the values of individual respect and equal entitlement inform the schooling system and its policies and practices. Thus, ultimately, when the system is informed and underpinned by a plurality of values. In his view, it is therefore necessary to go beyond the generalities of current debates and policies, and to specify a system of provision which entails at once attention to individual differences as well as to common entitlements, without preclusions to different forms of provision, both specialist and common, but with a broad commitment to inclusive values. As we have seen, Norwich further specifies his framework as a 'model of flexible interacting continua of provision' (page 105) where included and separate settings are coexisting in a balanced system. This flexible provision is organized along five dimensions. These include the identification of children's differences, elements of participation, curriculum and placement patterns, together with attention to factors of government and responsibility (page 105). Each dimension is further specified to include degrees of differentiation and commonality, according to different situations and contexts. For example, the curricular dimension is specified in three components, from a more differentiated dimension of common aims, but different pathways and specialized teaching approaches, to a more inclusive one, which entails the same aims and pathways for all, but with different teaching approaches (page 107). As Norwich notices, 'what is distinctive about this model is that it contains several dimensions of provision that are interconnected' (page 108), and hence the model does not focus solely on elements of placement, which seem to be the main, but ultimately limiting, concern of much debate about inclusive education. Furthermore, the model allows not only for the balancing of different elements, but also for a commitment to inclusive, common schools which respond appropriately and sensitively to children's differences. And it is ultimately this commitment which underpins Norwich's concerns, i.e. a concern about appropriate provision to be sought within the common school ideal, with the necessary attention to the specific and often unique needs of all children, as well as those of children designated as having special educational needs.

What emerges from this compelling discussion, ultimately, is that while the authors differ on their positions on separate provision and common entitlements, their perspectives nevertheless highlight and address crucially important questions about inclusive education. In her critique of the ideal, Warnock cogently reminds us that there are situations in which students with special educational needs receive an inadequate and, at times, detrimental education, and that this is morally unacceptable. Warnock also rightly points out that arguments in support of inclusive education cannot, and should not, be based on the idea that inclusion is valuable because it educates 'mainstream children' to understand and accept differences, since this amounts to undermining the dignity of children with special educational needs, who are entitled to equal respect and concern, and therefore to receive a good quality education. Furthermore, her perspective acts as an important reminder about the complex and often very specialized provision needed for children with severe and complex disabilities, and for those with critical illnesses, who are often neglected in the discussion, perhaps in virtue of the difficult questions arising in relation to their provision. What remains however open to further discussion, as highlighted and discussed by Norwich, is Warnock's complete rejection of the ideal of inclusion as related to the value of the common school, and, furthermore, her claim that schools should not be viewed as reflecting society's values and norms.

On the other hand, Norwich's perspective reminds us of the importance of recognizing and respecting differences, without losing sight of the fundamental aspects of commonality and equal entitlement. His position also provides a complex and articulated framework, where the highly debated issue of placement is considered in its relation to other, equally important elements. In his suggested system, special and 'hybrid' schooling arrangements co-exist with more inclusive ones. While many scholars supporting a notion of inclusive education as the absolute absence of special provision of any kind will find this suggestion unacceptable, Norwich's position seems helpful in delineating 'a system for developing a range of appropriate provision that matches a clearly specified inclusive framework' (page 79). What perhaps remains to be further debated at the level of ideals is Norwich's distinction between equality and respect, since this gives rise to questions about balancing the elements of both values, an issue that Norwich begins to address by admitting the necessity of appropriate political decisions, and by introducing an element of flexibility to his framework. At a more practical level, furthermore, some of the concerns expressed by Warnock in terms of carefully providing for children with severe and complex needs, and of providing contexts where these children can feel secure and confident to express themselves, may require some more specific elaboration, as does the question of ensuring commonality elements in separate settings. Several important questions, therefore, remain open to further research and discussion, as both Warnock and Norwich readily convene in their essays.

I have stated at the outset that the capability approach may offer some insights to the debate outlined so far, in addition to contributing to questions of identification of children's differences. Some considerations might therefore be helpful at this stage. In my view, perhaps the central concept relevant to the discussion of issues of inclusion is that of capability equality. The capability approach, as we have seen, defends a notion of equality in terms of the capabilities that people have to achieve valued functionings (the 'beings' and 'doings' that they value), thus to achieve well-being. It is against this 'currency' of fundamental human goods that the reciprocal position of individuals, their advantages and disadvantages, should be evaluated. The centrality of well-being in the approach parallels the importance that the approach assigns to the role of education in promoting well-being, and thus in equipping children to become equal participants in their social framework (see Terzi, 2008, for a more extensive articulation of this relation). The approach therefore suggests a conception of educational equality in terms of capability equality, or equal and genuine opportunities to achieve educational functionings fundamental to become active participants in society. What we owe to *all* children, the approach suggests, is an equal set of genuine opportunities to achieve educational functionings required to participate in society. Given its attention to human diversity, within this approach children with special educational needs, due to their possible restrictions in functionings, should receive additional and specific resources towards the aim of becoming social participants. Moreover, on the same bases, participating as equals in social arrangements entails typical and atypical functionings, thus ideally avoiding possible forms of discrimination, and does not presuppose specified norms of functionings either, therefore including diversity of modes of expression, socialization and contribution.

How can such a framework contribute to the debate on inclusive education? In my view, the centrality of the political notion of equality has some important theoretical and practical implications. First, such centrality shifts the focus of the debate from issues of location to issues of equality in provision, as well as quality of provision. To restate the principle at stake here, children with special educational needs should, as much as reasonably possible, receive the kind of education that enables them to achieve levels of functionings necessary to participate in society. This entails both elements of equal opportunities and quality of these opportunities. Second, the approach focuses on individuals' well-being and the expansion of agency, and these concepts might inform the analysis and the discussion about the question of placement for children with special educational needs, as well as about curricular elements. Whether the approach is consistent with a schooling system encompassing separate settings is an important question, which nevertheless requires much further analysis and research than these final comments.

On a practical level, enacting, through appropriate policies, a capability equality framework could help towards addressing the pervasive inequalities in resources which characterize current provision for children with special educational needs (see Introduction). This already would constitute an important step towards an improved educational provision, characterized by fair allocations of resources and opportunities for the enactment of best practice. Ultimately, discussing issues of inclusive education and provision for students with special educational needs or, indeed, for all vulnerable children in the light of the ideal of capability equality might add some important dimensions to the current debate. Each of these claims, however, admittedly requires further analysis and research.

A final thought, by way of a conclusion, is now due. The contributions to this volume have addressed some of the most difficult and controversial aspects of current educational theory and practice about provision for vulnerable children. Notwithstanding their differences in approaches and perspectives, the authors find a common voice in their expression of the moral concern for the well-being and the flourishing of these and all children.

References

Alkire, S. (2005), 'Needs and Capabilities' in Reader, S. (ed), *The Philosophy of Needs*. Royal Institute of Philosophy Supplement 57. Cambridge: Cambridge University Press.

Burchardt, T. And Vizard, P. (2007), 'Developing a Capability List: Final Recommendations for the Equalities Review Steering Group on Measurement'. CASE Series Paper April 2007.

Department for Education and Skills (2001a), *Special Educational Needs Code of Practice* (revised). London: DfES.

Department for Education and Skills (2001), *Special Educational Needs and Disability Act 2001*. London: HMSO.

Gutman, A. (1987), *Democratic Education*. Princeton: Princeton University Press.

Jayal, N., G. (2009), 'The Challenge of Human Development: Inclusion or Democratic Citizenship?'. *Journal of Human Development and Capabilities*10, 3, 359–74.

Pirrie, A. and Head, G. (2007), 'Martians in the Playground: Researching Special Educational Needs'. *Oxford Review of Education* 33, 1, 19–31.

Sen, A. (1984), *Resources, Values and Development*. Cambridge: Harvard University Press.

Sen, A. (1992), *Inequality Reexamined*. Oxford: Clarendon Press.

Sen, A. (2001), 'Social Exclusion: Concepts, Application and Scrutiny' *Social Development Papers No.1*. Manila: Office of Environment and Social Development, Asian Development Bank.

Terzi, L. (2005), 'Beyond the Dilemma of Difference: The Capability Approach on Disability and Special Educational Needs', *Journal of Philosophy of Education* 39 (3), 443–59.

Terzi, L. (2008), *Justice and Equality in Education. A Capability Perspective in Disability and Special Educational Needs*. London and New York: Continuum.

Terzi, L. (2009), 'Vagaries of the Natural Lottery? Human Diversity, Disability and Justice: a Capability Perspective'. In Brownlee, K. and Cureton, A. (eds) *Disability and Disadvantage: Re-Examining Topics in Moral and Political Philosophy*. Oxford: Oxford University Press.

Wedell, K. (2008), 'Evolving Dilemmas about Categorization' in Florian, L. and McClaughlin, M. (eds) *Disability Classification in Education: Issues and Perspectives*. Thousand Oaks: Corwin Press.

WHO (2007), *International Classification of Functioning, Disability and Health*. Geneva: World Health Organisation.

Index